KEY GEOGRAPHY

New
Basics

Tony Bushell

First published in 1999 by:
Stanley Thornes (Publishers) Ltd

This edition published in 2004 by:
Nelson Thornes Ltd
Delta Place
27 Bath Road
CHELTENHAM
GL53 7TH
United Kingdom

07 08 / 10 9 8 7 6 5 4

A catalogue record for this book is available from the British Library

ISBN 978 0 7487 7719 8

Page make-up by EMC Design
Illustrations by Jane Cope, Hardlines, Gordon Lawson, Richard Morris, Angela Lumley, Tim Smith and John York
Edited by Katherine James
Picture research by Penni Bickle and Liz Savery

Printed in Croatia by Zrinski

The previous page shows children of the Maasai tribe, Kenya

Acknowledgements

With thanks to the following for permission to reproduce photographs and other copyright material in this book:

Acestock 53C, 133B, 95B; Alamy 64Aiii; Art Directors and TRIP Photo Library 12B, 36B, 45E, 53D, 64Ai, 103B, 106A, 110A, 133C, 137D, 139Biii, 151C, 156A, 161C; Associated Press 22A; Tony Bushell 46A, 51D, 53F, 57B, 59B, 73C, 86A, 88-89A-H, 91A-C, 92, 104A, 140B; Corbis 133D, 133E; David Gardner 41C; Eye Ubiquitous 36D, 74A, 115Ei, 141D, 142C, 162A-D; Fiat 149D; Getty 133F; Holt 67B, 64Aiv, 73C; Hutchison Library 145D, 153D; Images of Africa Photobank/David Keith Jones 113 C & D; Impact Photos 97F, 115D, 143D; James Davis 44B, 108A, 142B, 150B, 154B; naturepl.com/Bernard Castelein 138ii; Oxford Scientific Films 115C; Pictures Colour Library 13C, 44C, 136A; Powerstock 133G; Q A Photos 38B; Rex Features 161D; Science Photo Library 47E; Still Pictures 21C, 23C & D, 36C, 49D, 74B & C, 109D, 111D, 114A, 115Eii & iv, 128A, 149C, 161F, 162E & F; The Travel Library 36A, 53E, 138Bi, 141C; Tokyo Metropolitan Government 155E; Topham Picturepoint 105C, 114B, 122A, 143E, 151D & E, 161E; Toyota 80A, 81C; Tony Waltham Geophotos 61C, 64Aii, 95B; Travel-Ink 13D; World Pictures 45D, 134A, 139ii; www.jasonhawkesaerial.com 49D; York Evening Press 17C.

The map extracts on pages 29, 49, 51, 56, 57, 78, 79, are reproduced from the 2003 1:50,000 Ordnance Survey map of Newcastle upon Tyne (Landranger 88), the 2001 1:25,000 Ordnance Survey map of Greenwich and Gravesend (Explorer 162), the 2002 1:25,000 Ordnance Survey map of South Devon Brixham to Newton Ferrers (Explorer OL20), the 2002 1: 50,000 Ordnance Survey map of Appleby-in-Westmoreland (Landranger 91) the 2002 1:50,000 Ordnance Survey map of Derby and Burton Upon Trent (Landranger 128). This product includes mapping data licensed from Ordnance Survey® with the permission of the Controller of Her Majesty's Stationary Office, © Crown copyright, Licence no. 100017284.

With thanks to the companies and organisations who have given permission for their logos to be used on pp. 75 and 152.

Every effort has been made to contact copyright holders. The publishers apologise to anyone whose rights have been inadvertently overlooked and will be happy to rectify any errors or omissions.

Contents

1 Weather and climate

What is Britain's weather?

Summer temperatures

Weather and climate are different. **Weather** is what happens day by day but **climate** is the average weather over many years.

Britain's climate varies from place to place and from season to season. Look at map **A** which shows temperatures around Britain in summer. Notice how different they are.

A

Summer temperatures in Britain

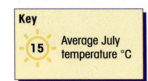

Key

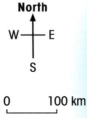
15   Average July temperature °C

North
W — E
S

0   100 km

Activities

1 Use the map to answer this question. Copy and complete the following sentences.
  a) The three warmest places in Britain are ......
  b) The three coolest places in Britain are ......

2 Write out the following sentences using the correct words from the brackets.
  a) Summer temperatures are (the same/not the same) all over Britain.
  b) The south is (warmer/cooler) than the north in summer.
  c) The north is (warmer/cooler) than the south in summer.

3 Find where you live on the map. Suggest what the temperature may be in summer.

There are many reasons why temperatures vary from place to place. The main one is that the sun does not give the same amount of heat all over the world.

Look carefully at diagram **B** below. It shows how the sun's heating effect is greater in some places than in others.

This helps explain why places near to the Equator are much warmer than places near to the north or south poles. It also explains why in summer, the south of Britain is warmer than the north.

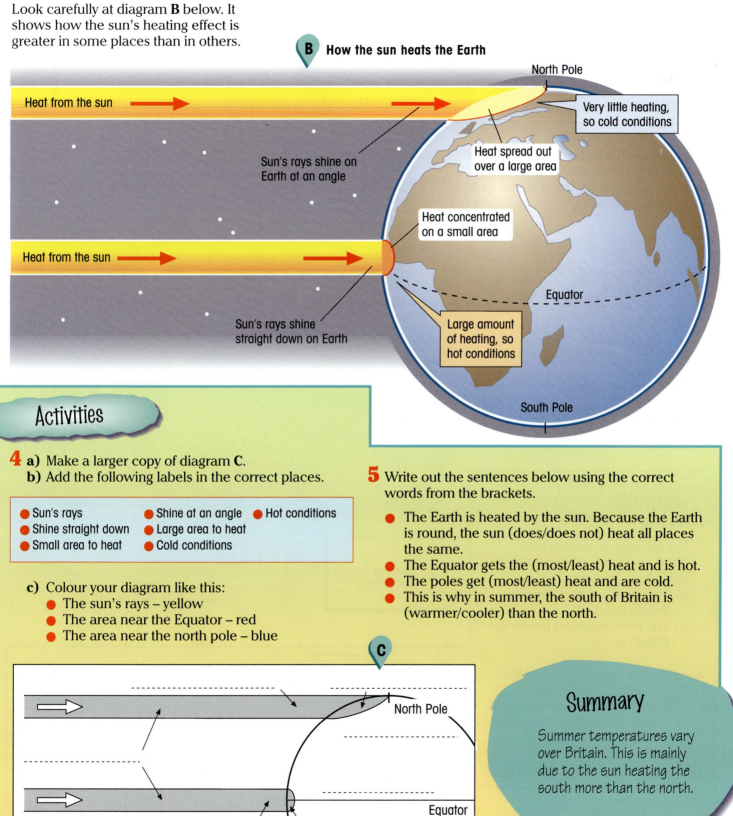

B How the sun heats the Earth

Heat from the sun

Sun's rays shine on Earth at an angle

Heat from the sun

Sun's rays shine straight down on Earth

North Pole

Very little heating, so cold conditions

Heat spread out over a large area

Heat concentrated on a small area

Equator

Large amount of heating, so hot conditions

South Pole

Activities

4 a) Make a larger copy of diagram **C**.
b) Add the following labels in the correct places.

- Sun's rays
- Shine straight down
- Small area to heat
- Shine at an angle
- Large area to heat
- Cold conditions
- Hot conditions

c) Colour your diagram like this:
- The sun's rays – yellow
- The area near the Equator – red
- The area near the north pole – blue

5 Write out the sentences below using the correct words from the brackets.

- The Earth is heated by the sun. Because the Earth is round, the sun (does/does not) heat all places the same.
- The Equator gets the (most/least) heat and is hot.
- The poles get (most/least) heat and are cold.
- This is why in summer, the south of Britain is (warmer/cooler) than the north.

C

North Pole

Equator

Summary

Summary temperatures vary over Britain. This is mainly due to the sun heating the south more than the north.

What is Britain's weather?

Winter temperatures

As we know, Britain is much colder in winter than it is in summer. But what is the pattern of temperature across the country? Is it the same as in summer – warmer in the south than in the north? Or is it different from that?

Look at map **A** which shows temperatures around Britain in winter. Where are the warmest places and where are the coldest? Can you see a pattern?

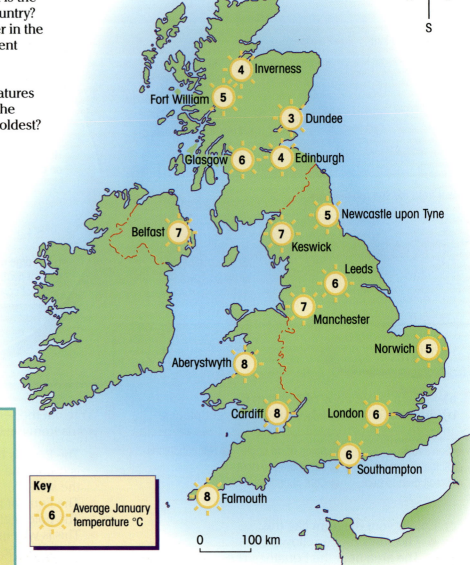

A Winter temperatures in Britain

North
W — E
S

Inverness **4**
Fort William **5**
Dundee **3**
Glasgow **6**   Edinburgh **4**
Newcastle upon Tyne **5**
Belfast **7**
7 Keswick
Leeds **6**
Manchester **7**
Norwich **5**
Aberystwyth **8**
Cardiff **8**   London **6**
6 Southampton
Falmouth **8**

Key

6 Average January temperature °C

0   100 km

Activities

1 Use the map to answer this question. Copy and complete the following sentences.
  a) The three coldest places in Britain are …
  b) The three warmest places in Britain are …

2 a) Make a copy of diagram **B**.
  b) Add either **warmer** or **colder** in the correct places.
  c) Colour the warmer box red and the colder box blue.

3 Find where you live on the map. Suggest what the temperature there may be in winter.

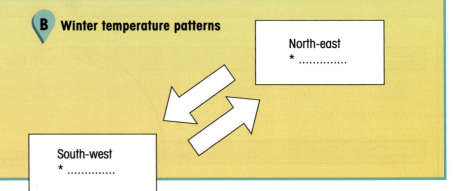

B Winter temperature patterns

North-east
* ....

South-west
* ....

Although Britain is cold in winter, it is not nearly as cold as many nearby countries. In fact geographers describe Britain's winter climate as **mild**.

The reason for this is a warm ocean current called the North Atlantic Drift. This current begins in the Caribbean as the Gulf Stream and flows some 7,000 kilometres across the Atlantic to warm Britain's shores. The effect of the warming is greater in the west than in the east.

Look carefully at map **C** which shows the effects of the North Atlantic Drift on sea temperatures.

C January sea temperatures

Key
Sea temperatures in °C
- Over 10
- 9–10
- 8–9
- 7–8
- 6–7
- 5–6
- Under 5

ATLANTIC OCEAN

NORTH SEA

Activities

4 Use map **C** above to answer this question. Copy and complete table **D** below. Choose your answers from this list:

Under 5°C   5–6°C   7–8°C   8–9°C   Over 10°C

D Differences in sea temperatures

a) Off the east coast	
b) Off the south-west coast	
c) Off the south-east coast	
d) The warmest part of the Atlantic	
e) The coldest part of the North Sea	

5 Find where you live on map **C**.
a) How will the North Atlantic Drift affect you?
- Will it warm you a lot?
- Will it warm you a little bit?
- Will it cool you down?
- Or will it have no effect?

b) Give a reason for your answer.

Summary

Winter temperatures vary over Britain. This is mainly due to a warm ocean current warming the west more than the east.

What is Britain's weather?

Rainfall

Britain receives a lot of rain. This is largely because it is an island surrounded by water. The main wind is from the west or south-west. From this direction the air passes over the Atlantic Ocean and picks up moisture. On reaching the land, this moisture often turns to rain.

Not everywhere in Britain receives the same amount of rain. Some places are very wet indeed whilst others are quite dry.

Look at map **A** which shows **rainfall distribution** across Britain. Where are the wettest places and where are the driest? Do you live in a wet area or a dry area?

Key

620 Rainfall in millimetres

North

W — E

S

0   100 km

A Annual rainfall in Britain

730 Inverness

Fort William 2000

790 Dundee

Glasgow 1560   699 Edinburgh

630 Newcastle upon Tyne

Belfast 846

1480 Keswick

Leeds 671

860 Manchester

Norwich 650

Aberystwyth 934

Cardiff 709   London 610

660 Southampton

1100 Falmouth

Activities

1 Use map **A** to answer this question.
   a) The five wettest places in Britain are ...
   b) The five driest places in Britain are ...

2 Which of the four maps in **B** best shows Britain's rainfall distribution?

3 Of the six sentences below, two are correct. Write out the correct ones.
   ● The south is wetter than the north.
   ● The east has more rain than the west.
   ● The east is drier than the west.
   ● The north is drier than the south.
   ● The west has more rain than the east.
   ● The west is drier than the east.

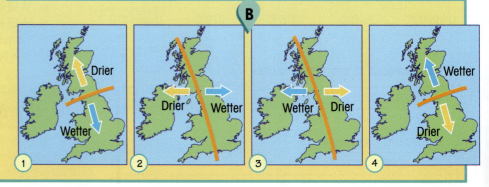

B

Drier / Wetter (1)

Drier / Wetter (2)

Wetter / Drier (3)

Wetter / Drier (4)

Rain occurs when moist air is forced to rise. This happens over high ground and explains why mountain areas are usually cloudier and wetter than lowland areas.

Map **D** shows that in Britain most of the high ground is in the west. The wind blows in from the west and is forced to rise over the mountains. This produces cloud and heavy rain. Rain like this is called **relief rainfall**.

Diagram **C** below explains relief rainfall and shows how some places are wet and some are dry.

C Relief rainfall in the north of England

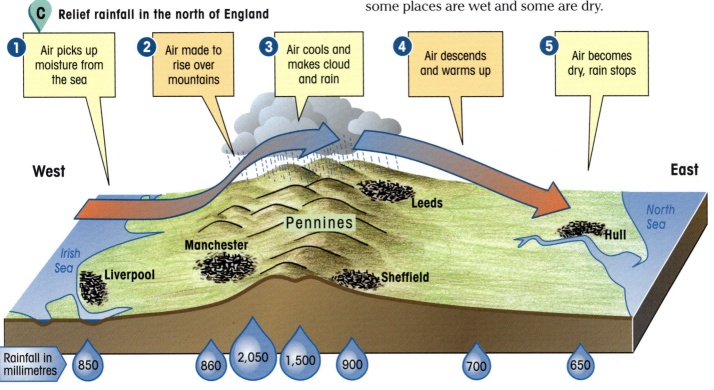

1 Air picks up moisture from the sea
2 Air made to rise over mountains
3 Air cools and makes cloud and rain
4 Air descends and warms up
5 Air becomes dry, rain stops

West · East

Leeds · North Sea · Pennines · Manchester · Hull · Irish Sea · Liverpool · Sheffield

Rainfall in millimetres — 850 · 860 · 2,050 · 1,500 · 900 · 700 · 650

Activities

4 Use diagram **C** to answer this question. Make a larger copy of drawing **E** below. Add these labels to the correct boxes.

Rain stops | Picks up moisture | Rises | Descends | Cloud and rain

E Relief rainfall

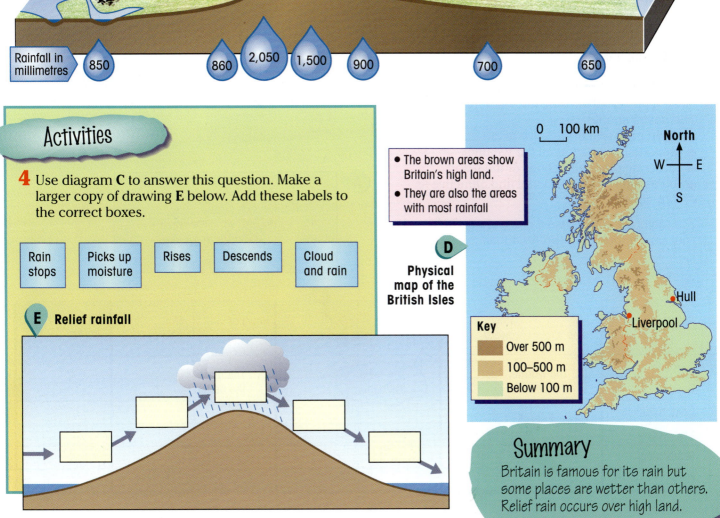

- The brown areas show Britain's high land.
- They are also the areas with most rainfall

D Physical map of the British Isles

Hull · Liverpool

Key
Over 500 m
100–500 m
Below 100 m

0   100 km

North W–E S

Summary
Britain is famous for its rain but some places are wetter than others. Relief rain occurs over high land.

What is Britain's weather?

Where to go on holiday

You are planning a summer holiday to a seaside resort in Britain with a friend. Both of you would like it to be warm and sunny with as little rain as possible. You know that the weather varies from one place to another so you will have to choose very carefully where to go.

Work with a partner on this task.

Activities

1 a) Make a copy of table **B** below.
b) Give the temperature for each resort. Award a star rating for each one, using box **A**.
c) Give the number of rainy days for each resort. Award star ratings.
d) Give the hours of sunshine for each resort. Award star ratings.
e) Add up the stars for each resort. The one with most stars should be best for your holiday.

Remember that in real life, other attractions are just as important as the weather.

2 Make a poster advertising the resort of your choice. The poster should:
- have a big and impressive resort name
- include information on the weather
- describe other attractions of the resort
- be as interesting, colourful and attractive as possible.

You might be able to use a computer to help make your poster look really professional.

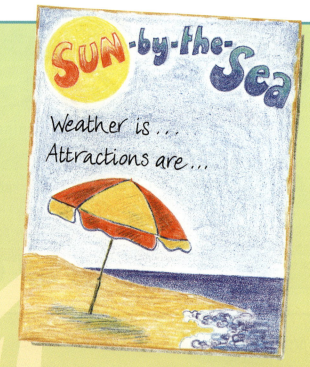

SUN-by-the-Sea

Weather is ...
Attractions are ...

A Star awards for weather

⭐⭐⭐⭐ Best
⭐⭐⭐ Second best
⭐⭐ Third best
⭐ Poorest

B

Resort	July temp.°C	Star award	Rainy days	Star award	Hours of sunshine	Star award	TOTAL STARS
Newquay							
Bournemouth							
Great Yarmouth							
Blackpool							
Scarborough							
Oban							

The warmer the better. The fewer the better. The more the better.

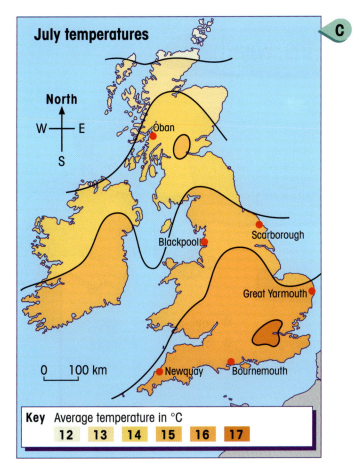

July temperatures C

Oban
Scarborough
Blackpool
Great Yarmouth
Newquay   Bournemouth

0   100 km

Key Average temperature in °C

| 12 | 13 | 14 | 15 | 16 | 17 |

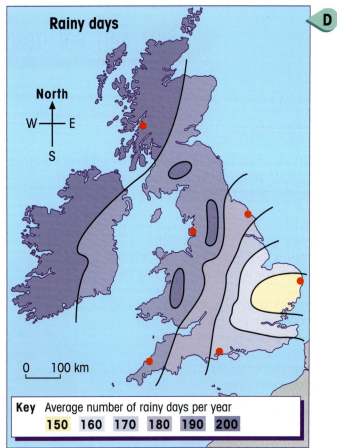

Rainy days D

0   100 km

Key Average number of rainy days per year

| 150 | 160 | 170 | 180 | 190 | 200 |

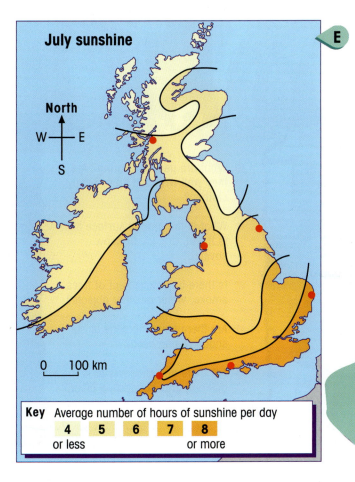

July sunshine E

0   100 km

Key Average number of hours of sunshine per day

| 4 | 5 | 6 | 7 | 8 |
| or less | | | | or more |

Summary

The weather over Britain varies from place to place. Weather maps help us compare the weather in different places.

How can we describe the weather?

We all know what the weather is. We experience it every day and it affects our lives in many different ways. But how can we describe the weather?

For a start we must look at all of the elements of weather. These include **temperature**, **precipitation**, **wind**, **visibility** and **general weather**.

For each of the elements we can then choose **key words** to describe the conditions at the time. Word Box **A** lists some of the key words that we may use.

Once the key words have been chosen, they can then be put into a series of sentences to describe the weather.

Describing the weather shown in a photo is slightly more difficult. To do this we need to be something of a detective and search for clues. Drawing **B** gives some tips on what to look for.

Words that help to describe or explain something that is important are called **key words**.

A

Word Box

hot	warm	cool	cold
frosty	freezing	icy	snowy
sunny	cloudy	dull	overcast
clear	misty	hazy	foggy
calm	light breeze	gusty wind	gales
dry	light showers	heavy rain	storm

B **London**

- What are people wearing? Are they well wrapped up or lightly clothed?

- What is the ground surface like? Is it wet, dry, icy or snow covered?

- Is there any movement of trees, smoke, water or other objects?

- Are there any umbrellas or sun shades being used?

- Are there any shadows or is it dull and grey suggesting cloud?

C Mallorca, Spain

D Northcliffe Hill, Shipley, West Yorkshire

Activities

E

Precipitation

Wind

Temperature

Visibility

General weather

1 Match each element of the weather in drawing **E** with the correct meaning below.
a) ...... is a measure of how hot or cold it is.
b) ...... includes rain, snow, sleet and hail.
c) ...... is the movement of the air.
d) ...... is the distance that can be seen.
e) ...... describes other weather features.

2 Write out a list of key words that describe the weather where you are at the moment. Choose the words from the Word Box.

3 Look carefully at photo **B**. Match the following clues with the correct weather statements.

People are wearing light clothes so	it is raining
People are using umbrellas so	there is little wind
The umbrellas are upright so	it is cloudy and overcast
There are no shadows so	it is quite warm

4 Write out the following sentences to describe the weather in photo **C**. Use the correct words from the brackets.

The weather in Mallorca is (hot/cool) and (cloudy/sunny). It is a (dry/cloudy) and (hazy/clear) day with a (light breeze/gusty wind).

5 Write a description of the weather shown in photo **D**.

Summary

There are five main elements to the weather. These can be described using key words.

2 River flooding

What causes a river to flood?

Flooding occurs when a river overflows its banks and covers the surrounding area with water. This happens when the river gets more water than it can hold. The flooded area is called a **flood plain**.

Floods are usually caused by heavy rain falling over a long period of time. Melting snow or ice can also cause rivers to flood. Drawing **A** shows how a flood happens.

A

Heavy rain or rapid snow melt

Water unable to soak into the ground

Water runs over the surface and into the river

River levels rise rapidly. River floods

Soil

Rock

How do rivers flood?

All rivers flood but some are more at risk than others. Heavy rain and anything that stops that rain from soaking into the ground will increase the risk of flooding. Some of the factors that prevent rain from soaking into the ground are shown below.

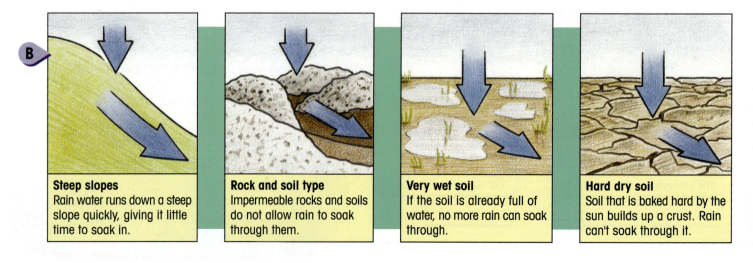

B

Steep slopes
Rain water runs down a steep slope quickly, giving it little time to soak in.

Rock and soil type
Impermeable rocks and soils do not allow rain to soak through them.

Very wet soil
If the soil is already full of water, no more rain can soak through.

Hard dry soil
Soil that is baked hard by the sun builds up a crust. Rain can't soak through it.

Floods are more common now than they used to be. There are more of them and they are increasing in size. Many people are blaming human activity for this.

Two ways in which humans may increase the risk of flooding are by cutting down trees and building towns and cities. These are shown below.

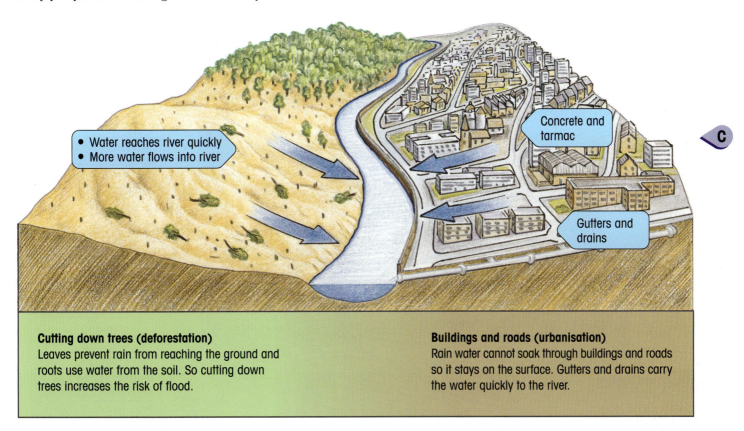

- Water reaches river quickly
- More water flows into river

Concrete and tarmac

Gutters and drains

C

Cutting down trees (deforestation)
Leaves prevent rain from reaching the ground and roots use water from the soil. So cutting down trees increases the risk of flood.

Buildings and roads (urbanisation)
Rain water cannot soak through buildings and roads so it stays on the surface. Gutters and drains carry the water quickly to the river.

Activities

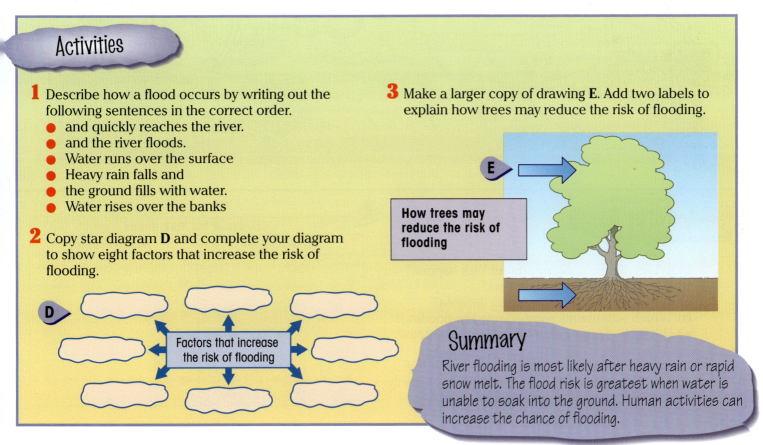

1 Describe how a flood occurs by writing out the following sentences in the correct order.
- and quickly reaches the river.
- and the river floods.
- Water runs over the surface
- Heavy rain falls and
- the ground fills with water.
- Water rises over the banks

2 Copy star diagram **D** and complete your diagram to show eight factors that increase the risk of flooding.

D

Factors that increase the risk of flooding

3 Make a larger copy of drawing **E**. Add two labels to explain how trees may reduce the risk of flooding.

E

How trees may reduce the risk of flooding

Summary

River flooding is most likely after heavy rain or rapid snow melt. The flood risk is greatest when water is unable to soak into the ground. Human activities can increase the chance of flooding.

15

Floods in the UK, 2000

Autumn 2000 was the wettest since records began in 1766. Major flooding affected large parts of the country. In some cases water levels were at their highest for over 100 years. One of the areas worst hit was the Vale of York in northern England.

The area around York has always been liable to flood. In recent times, however, flooding has occurred more often and been more serious than in the past. Many people blame human activity for this.

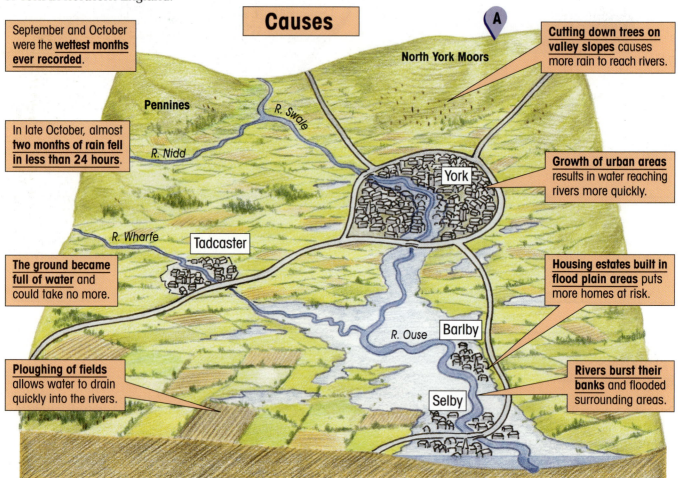

Causes

September and October were the **wettest months ever recorded**.

Cutting down trees on valley slopes causes more rain to reach rivers.

In late October, almost **two months of rain fell in less than 24 hours**.

Growth of urban areas results in water reaching rivers more quickly.

The ground became **full of water** and could take no more.

Housing estates built in flood plain areas puts more homes at risk.

Ploughing of fields allows water to drain quickly into the rivers.

Rivers burst their banks and flooded surrounding areas.

North York Moors
Pennines
R. Swale
R. Nidd
York
R. Wharfe
Tadcaster
R. Ouse
Barlby
Selby

Activities

1 a) When did the flooding around York happen?
   b) Which river flows through York?
   c) Which other three rivers drain the area?
   d) Which settlements were affected by flooding?
   e) What are the names of the two upland areas?

2 Use the information in drawing **A** to answer this activity. Copy and complete table **B**. You need only write in the words that are underlined.

B

Causes of the York floods	
Natural causes	Human causes
●	●
●	●
●	●
●	●

Effects

C

York floods: Autumn 2000

1 River levels in York highest for 375 years
2 Ouse at record high of 5.4 metres above normal
3 Seventeen severe flood warnings in place
4 Over a thousand properties flooded
5 Hundreds of people forced to leave their homes
6 Homes may take months to dry out
7 Several roads flooded and cars abandoned
8 Rail services cancelled or disrupted

9 Many shops, businesses and schools closed
10 Some businesses may never re-open
11 Large areas of countryside flooded
12 Farms cut off and boats used to move around
13 Crops destroyed by flood water
14 Farm animals trapped by rising water
15 Clean-up expected to take weeks
16 Insurance costs put at £200 million

D

3 Make a large copy of table **E**. Sort the statements from drawing **D** next to the correct headings in your table.
You need only write the number for each one. Some may be used more than once.

4 Look at photo **C**.
   a) Which statements in drawing **D** may describe features that you can you see in the photo?
   b) Write a description of the flood scene using the statements.

Effects of the flood   **E**

Facts and figures	
Main effects	
Effects on travel	
Problems after the flood	

Summary

There are usually several different causes of floods but some places are more at risk from flooding than others. Floods can cause much damage and seriously affect people's lives.

How does the UK cope with floods?

Most people think that flooding can never happen to them. Well it can. If you are one of the 5 million people in England and Wales who live on a flood plain your home is more likely to be flooded than it is to catch fire.

So how can we cope with floods and what can be done to reduce the danger and damage that they cause? The first thing to remember is that flooding can't always be prevented but it can be prepared for.

Rich countries like the UK are very fortunate. They can afford to support organisations and schemes that can help us prepare for flooding and reduce its damaging effects.

The **Environment Agency** is the organisation responsible for flood control in England and Wales. It builds and operates flood defences and issues flood warnings to the public. It also gives advice on how to prepare for a flood.

A

ENVIRONMENT AGENCY

Flood warning codes

Flood Watch means flooding is possible. Be aware! Be prepared! Watch out!

Flood Warning means flooding of homes, businesses and main roads is expected. Act now!

Severe Flood Warning means serious flooding is expected. There is imminent danger to life and property. Act now!

All Clear means there are no longer flood watches or flood warnings in place. Seek advice to return.

B

How to prepare for a flood

Be alert for flood warnings and take action.

Collect warm clothes, food and a torch.

Check on family and nearby neighbours.

Block doorways with planks or sandbags.

Move people, pets and valuables to safety.

Switch-off electricity and gas.

When there's a flood disaster the first aim is to make everyone safe. After that, there is a need to look after the victims and make them as comfortable as possible. Almost everyone helps in this. During the York flood of 2000, for example, help for the victims came from many different sources. A few of these are shown below.

C

Local schools and church halls provided shelter for those made homeless.

Volunteer groups gave support and reassurance to victims.

The Red Cross prepared tea and hot meals.

The Local Authorities provided caravans as temporary accommodation.

Supermarkets and shops gave free food, magazines and games.

The Army provided beds and bedding for the emergency shelters.

The Fire Service pumped out flood water from homes and businesses.

The police put on extra patrols to protect empty homes.

Activities

D

River levels rising. Heavy rain forecast.

Rain stopped. River levels dropping.

Heavy rain continues. River near top of bank.

River levels high. Rain approaching area.

1 Match up the flood warning codes in drawing **A** with the statements in **D**. Answer like this:

    Flood Watch = ...

2 You have to leave home because of flooding. List the items that you would put into an emergency bag for your own use. Try to include:
- 3 vital items you will need in the emergency
- 3 items that are valuable or important to you
- 3 items that you would like to have with you

3 Look at the information on drawing **C**. Name the organisations that helped victims of the York flood. Try to give at least eight.

4 Your school has to prepare for the arrival of flood victims. List the items you will need to make them comfortable.

Summary

There is no easy way to cope with floods. Rich countries like the UK can afford schemes that help reduce the damaging effects of flooding.

Floods in Bangladesh, 1998

Bangladesh is in Asia. It is located at the mouth of two of the world's longest rivers, the Ganges and the Brahmaputra. The country is very wet. It can get more rain in four months than London gets in two years. This makes flooding a big problem.

Bangladesh has heavy floods every year but in 1998 they were the worst ever. They lasted for over two months and more than two-thirds of the country was under water. The water in Dhaka was 2 metres deep. The effects were devastating.

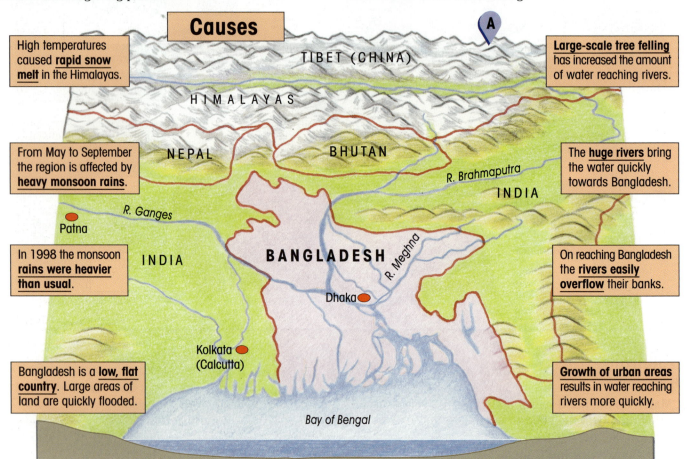

Causes

A

High temperatures caused **rapid snow melt** in the Himalayas.

Large-scale tree felling has increased the amount of water reaching rivers.

From May to September the region is affected by **heavy monsoon rains**.

The **huge rivers** bring the water quickly towards Bangladesh.

In 1998 the monsoon **rains were heavier than usual**.

On reaching Bangladesh the **rivers easily overflow** their banks.

Bangladesh is a **low, flat country**. Large areas of land are quickly flooded.

Growth of urban areas results in water reaching rivers more quickly.

TIBET (CHINA)

HIMALAYAS

NEPAL   BHUTAN

R. Brahmaputra

INDIA

R. Ganges

Patna

BANGLADESH

R. Meghna

INDIA

Dhaka

Kolkata (Calcutta)

Bay of Bengal

Activities

1 Complete these sentences.
   a) The country next to Bangladesh is ...
   b) The mountains north of Bangladesh are the ...
   c) The three rivers that flow into Bangladesh are ...
   d) The 1998 floods were the worst ever because ...

2 Use the information in drawing **A** to answer this activity.
Copy and complete table **B**. You need only write in the words that are underlined.

B

Causes of the 1998 Bangladesh floods		
Weather and climate causes	Physical causes	Human causes

Effects

C

D

Over 25 million people homeless

At least 2,379 people dead in floods

Millions threatened by disease and starvation

3 million farmers affected

Two-thirds of the country flooded

130 million cattle lost in killer flood

Fields washed away by waves of water

11,000 km of roads closed

More than 1,000 schools damaged

6,500 bridges damaged

Dhaka airport under water

3 Make a copy of the headlines in drawing **E**.
List the newsflashes from drawing **D** under the correct headlines.

4 Imagine that you are one of the people in photo **C**.
What would you find most difficult about the situation? Try to write down at least four things.

 E

Transport links broken as floods sweep country

Farmers hit as floods cover land

Worst ever floods hit Bangladesh

Summary

Most floods are caused by natural events but they can be made worse by human activity. Flooding can seriously affect people's lives.

How does Bangladesh cope with floods?

Bangladesh suffers more from flooding than any other country. The problem is made worse by the extreme poverty of the people who live there.

In 1989, several wealthy countries joined with Bangladesh to set up a Flood Action Plan. Under the plan, billions of dollars are being spent on schemes which it is hoped will reduce the risk and danger of flooding.

Look at map **B**, which shows the area around Kalni where flooding is a serious problem. Four different schemes have been suggested for the area. Your task is to decide which is the best scheme.

A Factors to consider	Scheme A	Scheme B	Scheme C	Scheme D
Prevents all flooding in area				
Stops flooding of main towns				
No bad effects elsewhere				
Saves people's lives				
Helps protect property				
Helps protect the land				
Rivers still accessible				
People able to work their land				
People don't have to move home				
Not too expensive				
Total				

Activities

1 a) Make a copy of table **A**. It shows some factors that have to be considered when choosing a flood protection scheme.

b) Look carefully at the map and scheme descriptions in drawing B.
- Show the advantages of each scheme by putting a tick in columns A, B, C or D.
- Complete one factor at a time.
- More than one column may be ticked for each factor.

c) Add up the ticks to find which scheme has the most advantages.

d) Which scheme would you choose? The one with the most advantages would be the best.

2 List the main features of the scheme that you have chosen.

3 Copy and complete the speech bubble below to show the advantages of the scheme.

> I like the scheme because .... and ....

Shop owner living in Kalni

Summary

Poor countries like Bangladesh find it very difficult to cope with floods. Some schemes can help reduce the risk and danger of flooding.

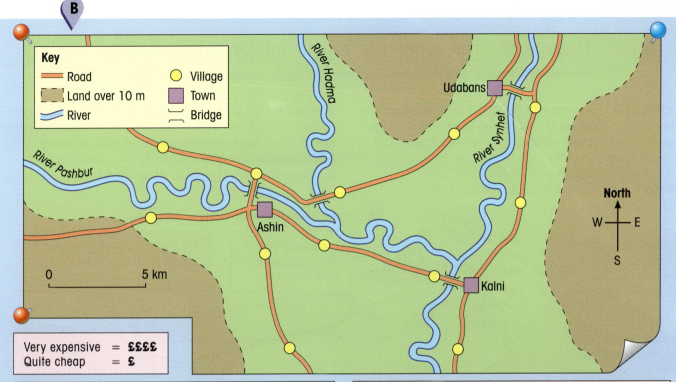

B

Key
- Road
- Land over 10 m
- River
- Village
- Town
- Bridge

River Hadma

River Pashbur

Udabans

River Synhet

Ashin

Kalni

North
W — E
S

0   5 km

Very expensive = £££££
Quite cheap   = £

Scheme A
Complete and strengthen embankments along main river channels. Build new embankments along all river banks where flooding is a problem.   **Cost = £££**

Scheme B
Move the towns and villages to higher ground. Re-route roads and build stronger bridges. Give earlier flood warnings.   **Cost = £££££**

Scheme C
Build embankments around main towns. Provide flood shelters for villages. Improve flood warning systems and rescue services.   **Cost = ££**

Scheme D
Improve flood warning systems and rescue services throughout the region. Build flood shelters in the areas most at risk.   **Cost = £**

C

Embankments protect people and property but make river access difficult. Too many can cause flooding downstream.

D

Flood shelters provide a place of safety for people and are cheap and easy to construct. They don't protect property or the land.

3 Settlement

How were the sites for early settlements chosen?

A **settlement** is a place where people live. Most people today live in settlements which began as small villages. Over the years, these villages have grown in size and are now towns and cities.

The place where a settlement was first built is called the **site**.

The site had to be chosen carefully if the people were to survive and the settlement was to grow. Early settlers spent much time choosing a place with as many advantages as possible. Some of the advantages of possible sites are shown in diagram **A** below.

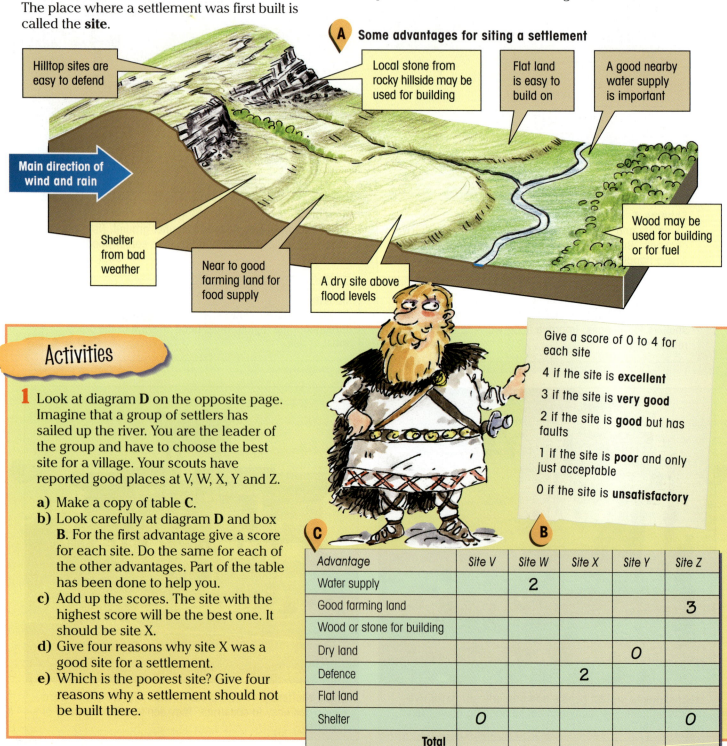

A Some advantages for siting a settlement

Hilltop sites are easy to defend

Local stone from rocky hillside may be used for building

Flat land is easy to build on

A good nearby water supply is important

Main direction of wind and rain

Shelter from bad weather

Near to good farming land for food supply

A dry site above flood levels

Wood may be used for building or for fuel

Activities

1 Look at diagram **D** on the opposite page. Imagine that a group of settlers has sailed up the river. You are the leader of the group and have to choose the best site for a village. Your scouts have reported good places at V, W, X, Y and Z.

a) Make a copy of table **C**.
b) Look carefully at diagram **D** and box **B**. For the first advantage give a score for each site. Do the same for each of the other advantages. Part of the table has been done to help you.
c) Add up the scores. The site with the highest score will be the best one. It should be site X.
d) Give four reasons why site X was a good site for a settlement.
e) Which is the poorest site? Give four reasons why a settlement should not be built there.

B

Give a score of 0 to 4 for each site

4 if the site is **excellent**

3 if the site is **very good**

2 if the site is **good** but has faults

1 if the site is **poor** and only just acceptable

0 if the site is **unsatisfactory**

C

Advantage	Site V	Site W	Site X	Site Y	Site Z
Water supply		2			
Good farming land					3
Wood or stone for building					
Dry land				0	
Defence			2		
Flat land					
Shelter	0				0
Total					

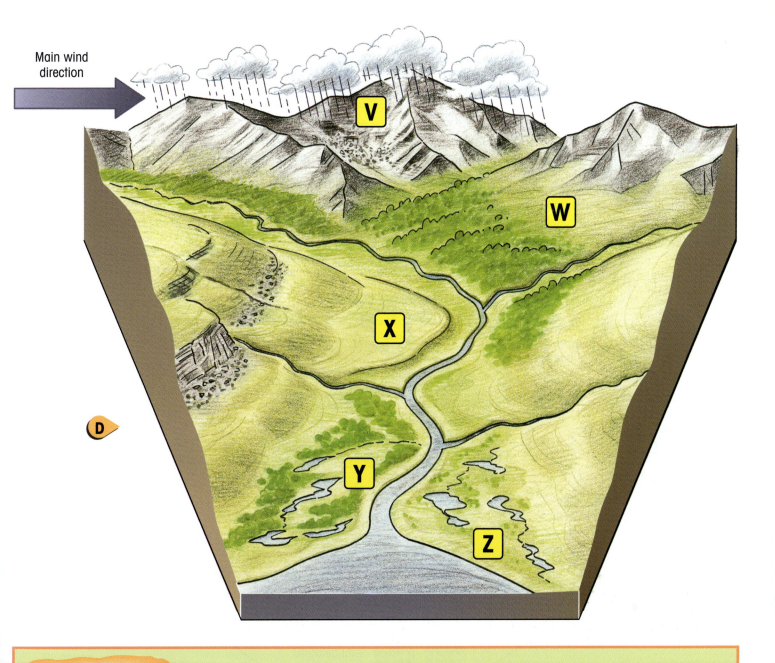

Main wind direction

V

W

X

Y

Z

Summary

Early sites for settlements had to be chosen carefully if they were to survive and grow. Advantages that were good for settlements include good water supply, dry land, shelter, building materials and farmland.

Activities

2 Complete the following by matching the beginnings on the left with the correct ending on the right.

A settlement	is important in times of trouble
A site	include wood and local stone
Building materials	is a place where people live
Defence	is usually a river and needs to be nearby
Farmland	is needed to produce food
Water supply	is the place where a settlement is built

3 Which advantages given in table **C** can be found in the settlement where you live? Give their names, e.g.
- Water supply – the River Thames
- Defence – Castle Hill

What is the pattern of land use in towns?

Most people in Britain now live in towns and cities. These are all very different. They may be industrial centres, ports, market towns or holiday resorts. Some places, like London, are very large with over a million people living in them. Others are much smaller and may have fewer than 100,000 inhabitants.

Although different in some ways, towns and cities all tend to be set out in a similar way. For example, the main shopping areas are found in the centre, and the newest housing is on the outskirts. Any industries are usually grouped together. If we look carefully at the layout of towns we can see that they are divided into areas or **zones**.

Diagram **A** shows these zones in a very simple way. It is called an **urban land use model**.

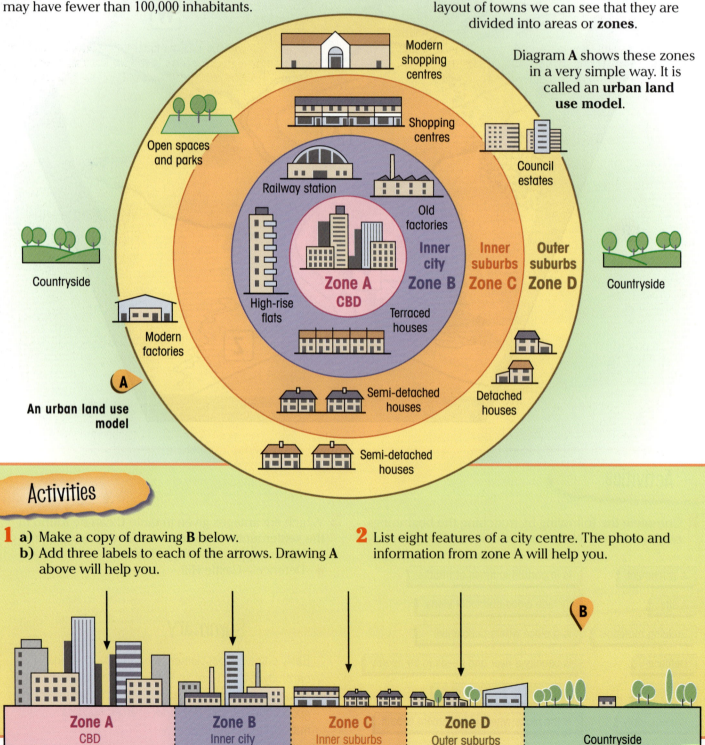

A An urban land use model

Activities

1 a) Make a copy of drawing **B** below.
b) Add three labels to each of the arrows. Drawing **A** above will help you.

2 List eight features of a city centre. The photo and information from zone A will help you.

| Zone A | Zone B | Zone C | Zone D | |
| CBD | Inner city | Inner suburbs | Outer suburbs | Countryside |

Zone A

The centre of town is called the **Central Business District** (**CBD** for short). This is where shops, offices, banks, public buildings and entertainments may be found. It is usually crowded and busy.

Zone B

Close to the town centre is the **inner city**. Factories and rows of terraced housing were built here in the last century. Many of the factories have now closed and the houses have been modernised.

Zone C

This area is called the **inner suburbs**. It is nearly all housing. Most are detached or semi-detached homes built in the 1920s and 1930s. Nearly all have gardens but there are few garages.

Zone D

The newest part of town is on the edge of the city. It is called the **outer suburbs**. Here are modern houses and council estates. There are also new shopping centres, small modern factories and areas of open space.

3 Copy and complete the chart below to describe the houses in zones B, C and D. Put a tick or a cross in each box. Two have been done to help you.

Zone	B	C	D
Terraced			
Semi-detached		✔	
In a row			
Bay window			
Garden			
Garage			
Very new	✗		

4 a) Describe the housing in zone B. Use the headings shown in the 'For Sale' sign.
b) Use the same headings to describe your own house.

FOR SALE

Type...
Age...
Building materials...
Design features...
Where it is...

Summary

Most towns have a similar pattern of land use and may be divided into zones. The names of these zones are the CBD, inner city, inner suburbs and outer suburbs. Most people live in the suburbs.

How can maps show patterns of land use?

Maps give information and show where places are. Ordnance Survey (OS for short) maps are very accurate and give information for the whole of the UK. By looking at an OS map very carefully, we can find out about land use both in countryside areas and in towns.

The map opposite shows part of Newcastle upon Tyne in northern England. The key and scale below the map help us measure distance and understand the symbols used on the map.

Activities

1 Copy and complete the sentences below by using the OS map key.
a) The symbol for a church with a tower is ▮
b) The symbol for a golf course is ...
c) The symbol for a motorway is ...
d) The symbol for a main road is ...

2 Look at Mapskills 1 and the OS map. Copy and complete the sentences below by putting the correct grid reference in the space. Choose your answers from this list:

| 2168 | 2065 | 2369 | 2564 |

a) The church with a tower is in grid square **2065**
b) The golf course is in grid square ......
c) The motorway is in grid square ......
d) The main road is in grid square ......

3 Make a larger copy of the table below. Complete the table as follows.
a) Name the land use zone for each reference. See the purple dashed lines on the map.
b) Give the location for each zone. Choose from:

Close to centre   Edge of city

City centre   Next to outer suburbs

c) Describe the street pattern for each zone. Choose from:

Complicated   Open grid

Curved streets   Tight grid

d) Describe the amount of open space. Choose from:

Very little   Quite a lot   Some   Little

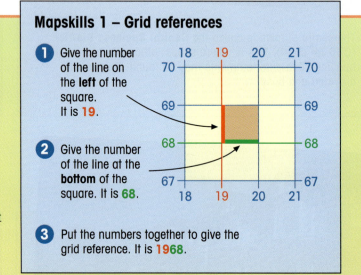

Mapskills 1 – Grid references

1 Give the number of the line on the **left** of the square. It is **19**.

2 Give the number of the line at the **bottom** of the square. It is **68**.

3 Put the numbers together to give the grid reference. It is **1968**.

Grid reference	Name of zone	Location of zone	Street pattern	Open space
2464				
2264				
2065				
1867				

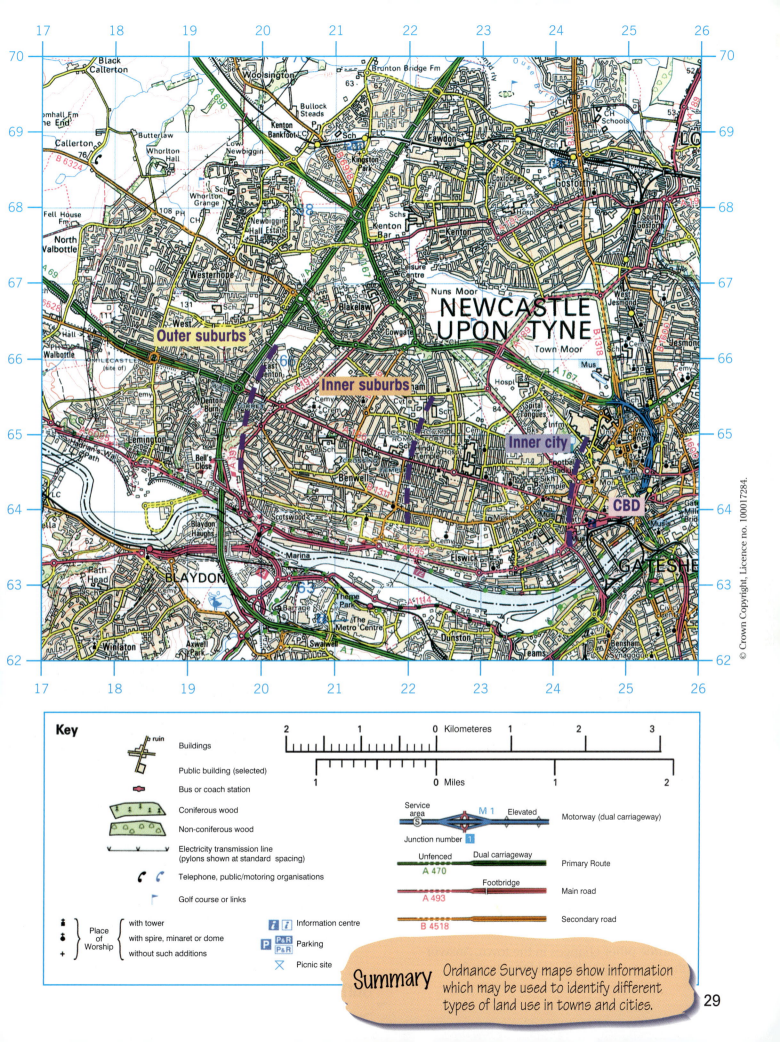

Key

- Buildings
- Public building (selected)
- Bus or coach station
- Coniferous wood
- Non-coniferous wood
- Electricity transmission line (pylons shown at standard spacing)
- Telephone, public/motoring organisations
- Golf course or links
- Place of Worship { with tower / with spire, minaret or dome / without such additions }
- Information centre
- Parking
- Picnic site

Kilometeres: 2 1 0 1 2 3

Miles: 1 0 1 2

- Service area
- Junction number
- Elevated
- Motorway (dual carriageway) M 1
- Unfenced / Dual carriageway — Primary Route A 470
- Footbridge — Main road A 493
- Secondary road B 4518

NEWCASTLE UPON TYNE

Outer suburbs
Inner suburbs
Inner city
CBD

BLAYDON
GATESHEAD

© Crown Copyright, Licence no. 100017284.

Summary Ordnance Survey maps show information which may be used to identify different types of land use in towns and cities.

29

How does land use in towns change?

Towns and villages change as the years go by. These changes happen because settlements grow and people's needs change.

Sometimes buildings have to be knocked down. This may be because they are simply too old, unsuitable for modern use, or in the way of new developments.

At other times new buildings may be needed. These could be to house more people or to provide things that we need, like shops and health care.

Often the change is small. A building may just have a change of use or need to be modernised.

The two drawings on the opposite page show a typical town. See how many changes you can spot.

Activities

1 Find at least ten differences between the town in the 1960s and the same town in the year 2000.

2 Match the features below with the correct grid squares.
Answer like this: **E10 is a shopping parade.**

B4 is ......   A3 is ....   G2 is ....
B2 is ....   C7 is ....

Terraced housing

Shopping parade

Detached housing

Shopping superstore

High school

Semi-detached housing

3 Copy and complete these sentences to show how land use has changed in the town. The first one has been done for you.
a) Parkland (E3) changed to **new road** (E8)
b) School fields (A2) changed to ...... (A7)
c) Farmland (F1) changed to ...... (F6)
d) Fields (C2) changed to ...... (C7)
e) ...... (E4) changed to high rise (E9)
f) ...... (G3) changed to new road (......)

4 Give three other changes in the town. Answer in the same way as you did for activity **3**.

5 Give the grid square for the improvements below. The first one has been done for you.
a) Old factory knocked down **B10**.
b) New shopping superstore opened ......
c) Modern housing estate built ......
d) Terraced housing improved ......
e) Road widened ......
f) New cinema opened ......

6 The people below live in grid squares C3 and C8. Complete the speech bubbles to describe the effects of land use change in that part of town.

This was a good place to live in the 1960s because .... and ....

It's not so good now because .... and ....

Summary As time passes, the land uses of different parts of a town will change. These changes may affect people in different ways.

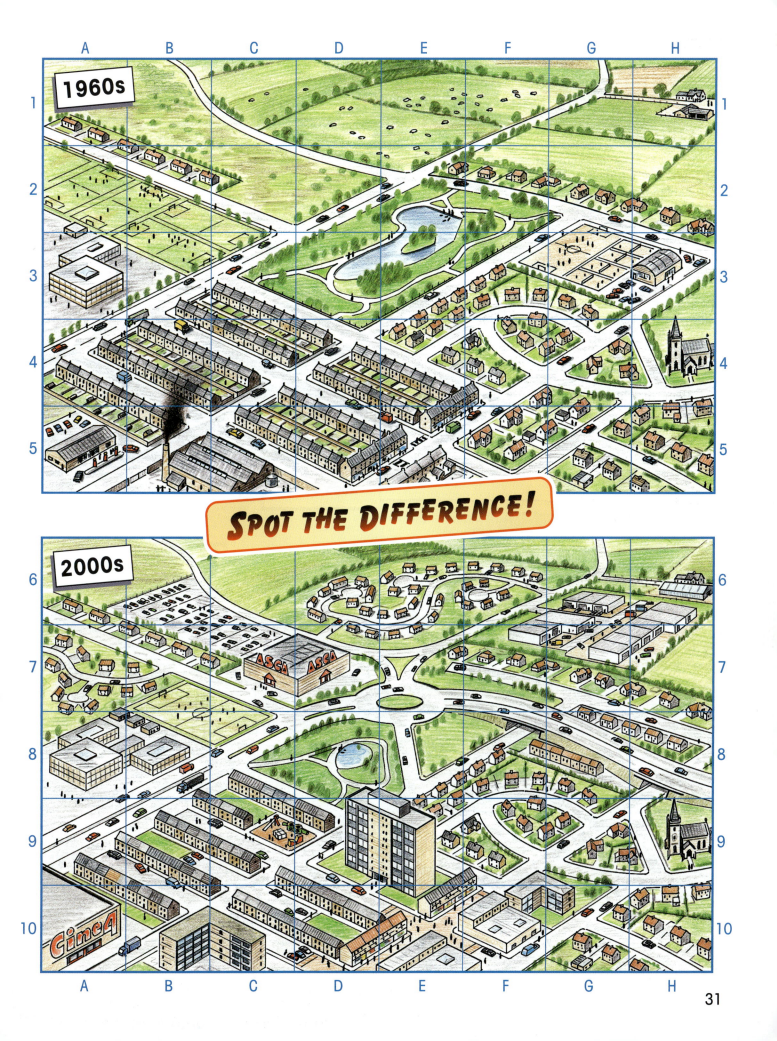

How can changes in land use affect people?

No town or village remains the same for ever. Changes are happening all the time. Most are carefully planned and aimed at improving the **quality of life** in a place.

However, changes can affect different groups of people in different ways. What is good for some people is not always good for others.

Planners have to try to decide how land should be used so that it brings the greatest benefit to the greatest number of people. This is often difficult.

Look at drawings **B** and **D** below which show **conflict** between people over plans for a new road. Conflict is disagreement.

Activities

Work in pairs or in a small group for these activities. This will help you share other people's ideas and views.

1 Use drawing **B** to answer this activity. Copy and complete table **A** below. You need only write the words that are underlined on the drawing.

A

Bad things about old roads	Good things about new roads
●	●
●	●
●	●
●	●

B Road users

32

2 Use drawing **D** to answer this activity. Copy and complete drawing **C** below. Choose the **six** problems **you** think are the worst. You need only use the words written in red.

C

Worries of local residents

3 Discuss each of the following statements. Answer **yes** or **no** to each one. Give a reason for your answer.
- **Planner** A new road would be good for everyone.
- **Public safety officer** A wider road would be safer.
- **Local children** A new road would be bad for us.
- **Business people** Better roads help business.
- **Local shopkeepers** Faster roads are good for us.

4 Copy and complete the following sentence. Choose from the words given in brackets. Give reasons for your choice.
- A new road (would/would not) be good because ....
and ....

Summary   Changes in land use affect people in different ways. Sometimes the changes can cause problems for people.

Local residents D

Traffic in urban areas – what is the problem?

Towns and villages are constantly changing. One of the biggest changes is due to the increase in car ownership. Large cities such as London have over a million cars trying to move around in their central areas.

The problem is worst during the **rush hour** when people are going to work and returning home. Movement at this time is often almost impossible.

Most people agree that traffic is spoiling our cities. It brings congestion, pollution and danger. It also damages the environment and, for many people, makes the city an unattractive place to be.

Activities

Work in pairs or in a small group for these activities. This will help you share other people's ideas and views.

1 Use drawing **B** to answer this activity. For each of the people below, list the transport problems that you think will most affect them. You need only write the headings that are in **red**.

Car driver   Pedestrian   Shop owner

Traffic jams block roads and can stop all movement of vehicles.

Delays affect public transport and emergency services.

Exhaust fumes are poisonous and a danger to health.

Accidents kill or injure hundreds of people each year.

Cities for cars, or … ➤

A

Noise and vibrations affect people and buildings.

Shops lose money as fewer customers travel into the city.

Time is wasted as people spend hours sitting in traffic jams.

Car parking takes up huge areas of space in overcrowded cities.

2 Use drawing **C** to answer this activity.
- Arrange the statements in a diamond shape as shown in drawing **B**.
- Put the improvement you like best at the top.
- Put the next two below, and so on.
- The improvement you like least will be at the bottom.
- You need only write the words printed in **bold**.

3 Copy and complete the speech bubble below.
Give at least two improvements.

The improvements I would most like to see in the city are ....
This is because ....

Summary

Congestion and pollution are major problems in urban areas. Reducing traffic can help improve the city environment.

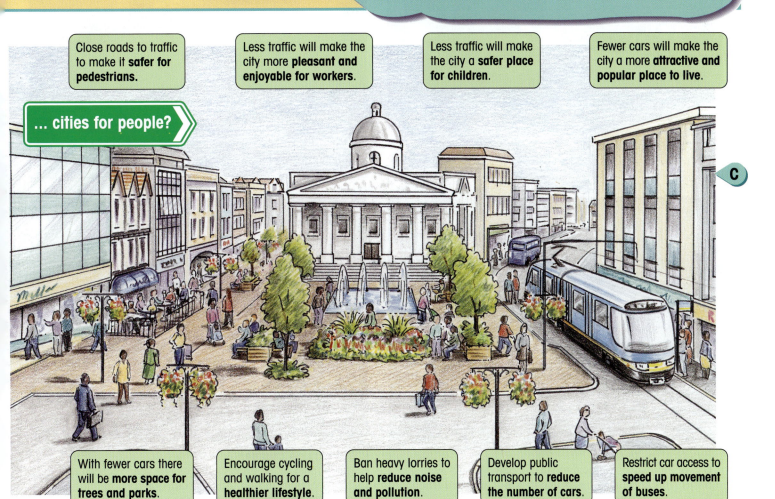

Close roads to traffic to make it **safer for pedestrians**.

Less traffic will make the city more **pleasant and enjoyable for workers**.

Less traffic will make the city a **safer place for children**.

Fewer cars will make the city a more **attractive and popular place to live**.

... cities for people?

With fewer cars there will be **more space for trees and parks**.

Encourage cycling and walking for a **healthier lifestyle**.

Ban heavy lorries to help **reduce noise and pollution**.

Develop public transport to **reduce the number of cars**.

Restrict car access to **speed up movement of buses**.

Traffic in London – is there a solution?

London is the UK's largest city. It has the most people and covers the biggest area. It also has the most cars and the worst traffic problems.

Attempts to solve the problems by improving the flow of traffic have largely failed. New roads and better junctions have encouraged more cars and led to even greater congestion and pollution.

The aim of the new transport plan for London is to try and reduce car numbers. There are two ways of doing this. The first is to provide better public transport. This encourages people to use buses and trains rather than cars. The second is to discourage motorists from bringing their cars into the city.

Some ways of doing this are shown below.

A

Improve public transport
Make buses and trains cheaper, cleaner, quicker and more reliable. This will increase their use and reduce the need to use cars.

B

Park and ride schemes
Motorists use free car parks on the edge of town and continue their journey by public transport. This reduces the number of cars in the city centre.

C

Bus priority lanes
One or more lanes of main roads can only be used by buses. This speeds up buses and makes them more reliable. It slows down cars and so discourages their use.

D

Car parking changes
The number of car parking spaces has been reduced and the charges increased. This discourages car use and increases the use of public transport.

Another way of discouraging motorists from using their cars is by **congestion charging**. This was introduced to London in 2003. In this scheme, motorists are charged £5 a day to enter London's central zone. A network of over 800 cameras sited on the boundary and throughout the zone read car number plates. Computers then check for payment and fines are issued where necessary. Although the scheme has many advantages, some people are against it.

E

Profits are used to improve public transport.

Traffic just outside the charge area has increased.

Traffic in the area has been reduced by up to 15%.

It is unfair to less well off people who can't afford to pay.

Less congestion is saving businesses up to £2 million a week.

It is costing people more money to travel to work by car.

The quality of life for people in the area is much improved.

Extra costs have forced some people to leave their jobs.

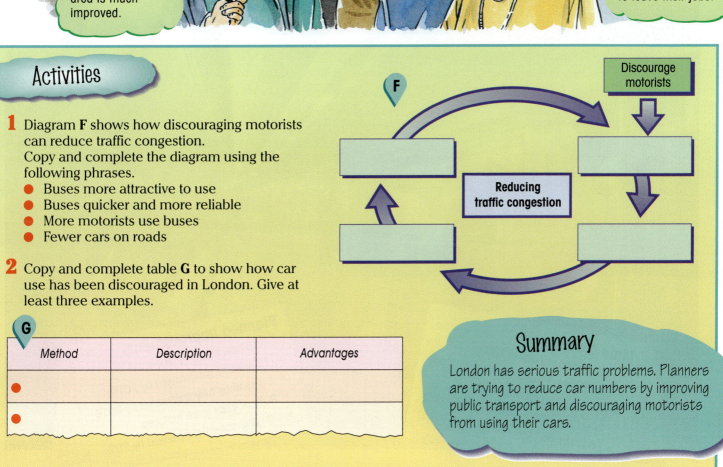

Activities

1 Diagram **F** shows how discouraging motorists can reduce traffic congestion.
Copy and complete the diagram using the following phrases.
● Buses more attractive to use
● Buses quicker and more reliable
● More motorists use buses
● Fewer cars on roads

2 Copy and complete table **G** to show how car use has been discouraged in London. Give at least three examples.

F

Discourage motorists

Reducing traffic congestion

G

Method	Description	Advantages
●		
●		

Summary

London has serious traffic problems. Planners are trying to reduce car numbers by improving public transport and discouraging motorists from using their cars.

Traffic in London – the Underground

The London Underground is one of the oldest and largest subway systems in the world. It carries millions of passengers a day. This means that there is less traffic on the roads. Some of the advantages of the London Underground as a form of transport are shown in drawing **A**.

The Underground, or Tube as it is also known, is now very old. Many people complain about standards of comfort, cleanliness, safety and reliability.

A modernisation programme is now underway. The aim is to improve the quality of travel and encourage more people to use the system. This will help reduce traffic congestion even more.

A

Advantages
- Separate from cars
- Not held up by traffic jams
- Quicker than road travel
- Reduces air pollution
- Safer than road travel
- Covers a large area
- Reduces car use
- Links to railway stations and airport

B

Main features
- First section opened in 1863
- Carries over 3 million passengers a day
- 267 stations presently in use
- Total track length 392 km (244 miles)
- Underground track 167 km (105 miles)

Planned improvements
- 336 new trains by 2014
- 70 stations modernised by 2010
- Trains to be fully automated by 2016
- 80% of track to be replaced
- Carrying capacity increased by 20%

Map **C** shows part of the London Underground. To make it easier to read it has been drawn with as many straight lines as possible.

You will notice that many different colours are used. These colours show different lines on the Underground. To transfer from one line to another you must use an interchange station (O).

C The London Underground

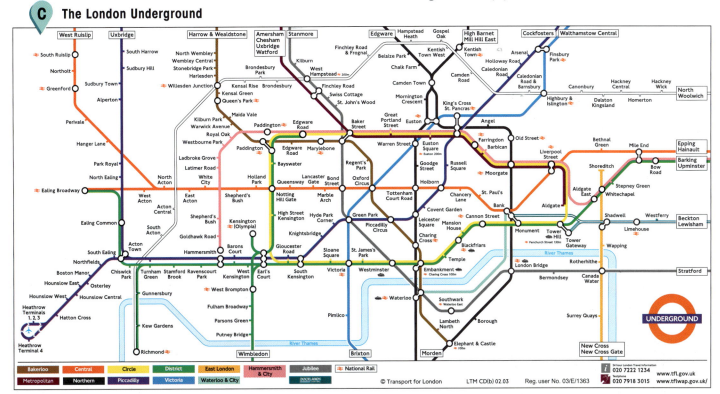

Activities

1 Copy and complete these sentences.
  a) Another name for the Underground is ...
  b) The Underground first opened in ...
  c) The number of passengers carried is ...
  d) Four advantages of the Underground are ...
  e) Improvements will help ...

2 Look at map **C** of the London Underground. Name the lines at the stations below.
Answer like this:
1 Bond Street = Central and Jubilee lines

1 Bond Street	**2** Piccadilly Circus
3 Victoria	**4** Oxford Circus
5 Notting Hill Gate	**6** Leicester Square

3 a) Name two stations that have one line only.
  b) Name two stations that have two lines.
  c) Name two stations that have three lines.
  d) Which station has most lines? Name the lines.

4 Name the stations on the journeys below.
Answer like this:
1 Oxford Circus to Queensway – Bond Street, Marble Arch and Lancaster Gate.

1 From Oxford Circus to Queensway
2 From Victoria to Marble Arch
3 From South Kensington to Piccadilly Circus
4 From Green Park to Wembley Park
5 From Bond Street to Waterloo

Summary

The London Underground is a rail-based public transport system. It is a quick way of travelling and can help reduce congestion and pollution.

Where should the by-pass go?

Look at drawing **B**. It shows the area around Burniston, a small village near Scarborough in North Yorkshire.

The amount of traffic passing through Burniston has increased rapidly in the last few years. This has brought congestion and pollution to the village. There have also been many accidents.

In a recent survey, 96% of the villagers felt that there was too much traffic. Planners suggested that a **by-pass** could help reduce the problem. A by-pass is a road that takes traffic around busy areas.

Several routes for a possible by-pass have now been surveyed. Choosing the best route can be quite difficult and can take a long time.

Activities

Drawing **B** shows three possible routes for a by-pass around Burniston. Your task is to choose the best one.

Considerations	Blue route	Red route	Yellow route
Is the shortest route			
Avoids all the built-up area			
Joins with the A171 in north			
Joins with the A171 in south			
Joins with the A165			
Avoids beauty spot			
Avoids National Park			
Follows existing road			
Follows route of old railway			
Avoids cycle routes			
Total			

A

1 a) Copy table **A**.
   b) Show advantages of each route by putting a tick in the Blue, Red or Yellow columns. More than one column may be ticked for each point.
   c) Add up the ticks to find which route has the most advantages.
   d) Which route would you choose? The one with the most advantages would be best.

2 Copy and complete these sentences.
   ● The best route is ....
   ● Two advantages of this route are ...
   ● One disadvantage of this route is ...

3 Complete the speech bubbles to show two different views of the Yellow route.

I'm in favour of the Yellow route because .... and ....

I'm against the Yellow route because .... and ....

Tom Woods
National Park Ranger

Jane Pounds
Finance Department Officer

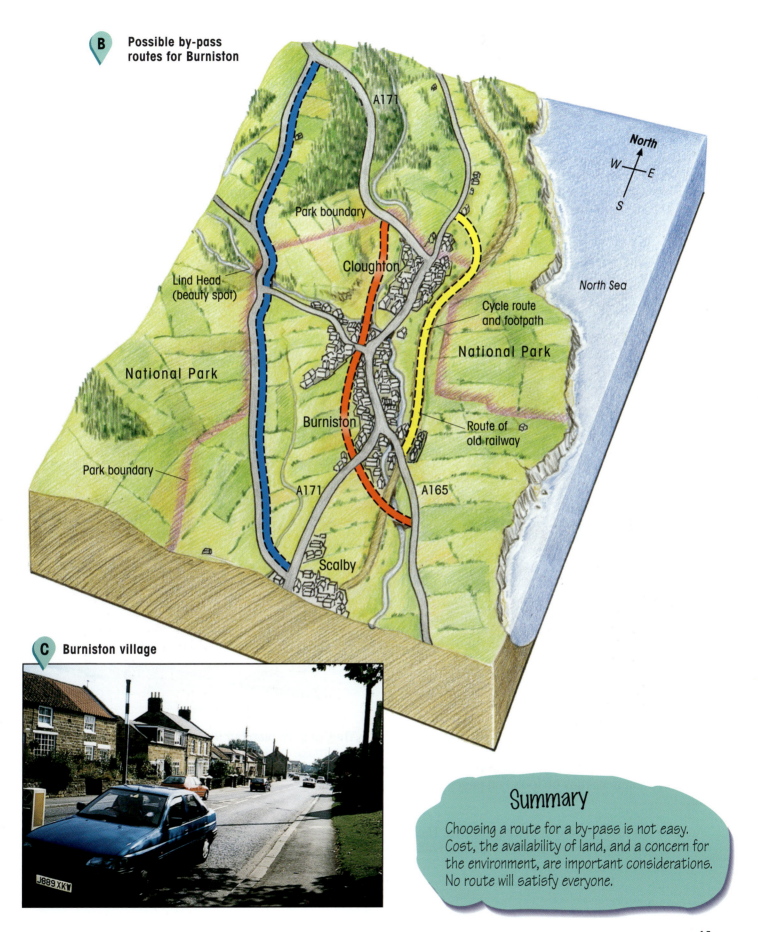

B Possible by-pass routes for Burniston

A171

North

W — E

S

Park boundary

North Sea

Lind Head (beauty spot)

Cloughton

Cycle route and footpath

National Park

National Park

Burniston

Park boundary

Route of old railway

A171

A165

Scalby

C Burniston village

Summary

Choosing a route for a by-pass is not easy. Cost, the availability of land, and a concern for the environment, are important considerations. No route will satisfy everyone.

Should the by-pass be built?

Towns and villages are changing all the time. Most changes are carefully planned and aimed at improving the **quality of life** in a place.

However, changes can affect different groups of people in different ways. What is good for some people is not always good for others. This can cause **conflict**. Conflict is disagreement.

Building a by-pass is not easy and often causes conflict. Money has to be found and suitable routes planned out. Discussions must then be held between people whom the route may affect.

Drawing **A** shows a meeting where views on the Burniston by-pass from pages 40 and 41 are being discussed. Once the various views have been heard, a considered decision about the by-pass can be made.

A by-pass will make the village **quieter and more pleasant**.

The by-pass will **increase traffic, noise and pollution**.

A by-pass will **make travel easier**.

Our **shops will lose trade** and may close.

New roads are **safer for drivers and pedestrians**.

Some areas of the **countryside will be spoilt**.

I'll **get home quicker** and have more time with the family.

Our **houses will be knocked down** for the by-pass.

Writing frames

Writing can be made easier if it is well planned and has a good structure. **Key questions**, **key words** and **key sentences** can help us do this. Examples of key words and key sentences may be found on pages 12, 52 and 72.

Another approach is to use **writing frames**. These provide a framework on which to base our writing.

They help us plan our sentences and paragraphs. They also make sure that we keep closely to the topic or issue that we are studying.

Drawing **B** is a writing frame. We can use it to put the arguments for and against the Burniston by-pass. It can then help us suggest the best outcome.

B

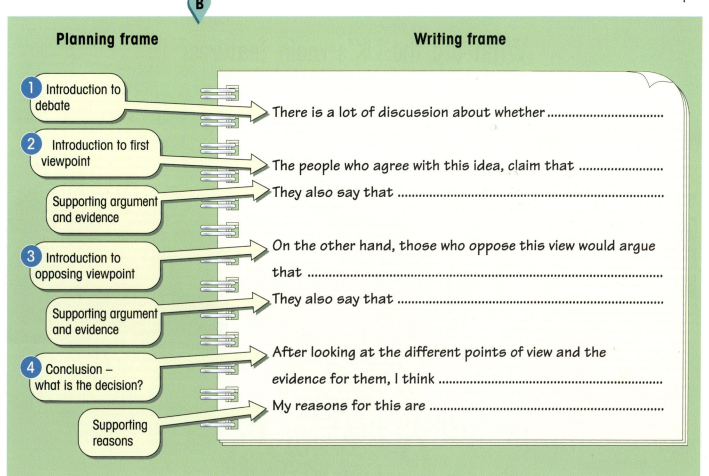

Planning frame

1 Introduction to debate

2 Introduction to first viewpoint

Supporting argument and evidence

3 Introduction to opposing viewpoint

Supporting argument and evidence

4 Conclusion – what is the decision?

Supporting reasons

Writing frame

There is a lot of discussion about whether ....

The people who agree with this idea, claim that ....
They also say that ....

On the other hand, those who oppose this view would argue
that ....
They also say that ....

After looking at the different points of view and the
evidence for them, I think ....
My reasons for this are ....

Activities

Work in pairs or in a small group for these activities. This will help you to share other people's views and ideas.

1 **a)** Make a large copy of table **C**.
　b) Look at drawing **A** and list the advantages and disadvantages of the by-pass. You need only write the words that are underlined in the drawing.
　c) Discuss the importance of each advantage and disadvantage. Give a score of 1 to 4 for each.

2 **a)** Decide as a group whether you are **for** or **against** the by-pass.
　b) Write a report on the issue using the writing frame in drawing **B**.

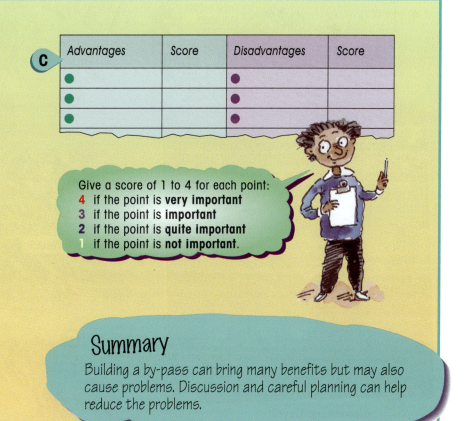

C

Advantages	Score	Disadvantages	Score
●		●	
●		●	
●		●	

Give a score of 1 to 4 for each point:
4 if the point is **very important**
3 if the point is **important**
2 if the point is **quite important**
1 if the point is **not important**.

Summary

Building a by-pass can bring many benefits but may also cause problems. Discussion and careful planning can help reduce the problems.

What are the UK's main features?

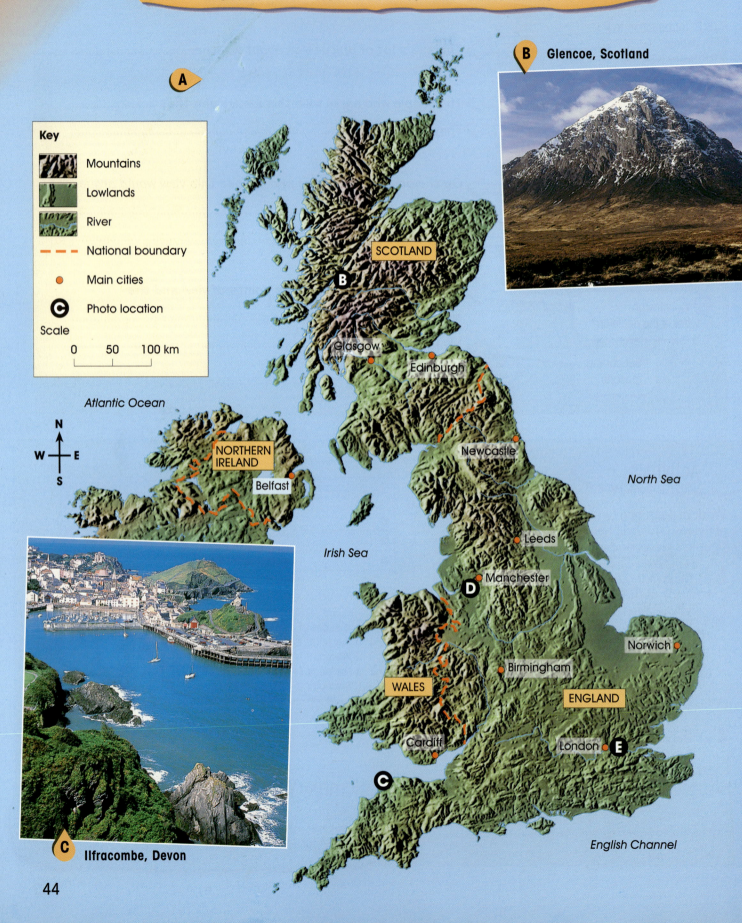

B Glencoe, Scotland

Key

	Mountains
	Lowlands
	River
– – –	National boundary
●	Main cities
C	Photo location

Scale

0   50   100 km

Atlantic Ocean

A

B

SCOTLAND

Glasgow

Edinburgh

N
W ✦ E
S

NORTHERN
IRELAND

Belfast

Newcastle

North Sea

Irish Sea

Leeds

D Manchester

WALES

Birmingham

Norwich

ENGLAND

Cardiff

London **E**

C

C Ilfracombe, Devon

English Channel

This is the United Kingdom as seen from space. National boundaries and some of the main cities have been added.

Look carefully at the map and key. Notice that the mountains are mainly in the north and west. The south and east is flatter with low hills and rolling plains. Some of the longest rivers can also be seen. How many can you count?

The UK is a small but crowded country with a population of about 60 million. Most people live in the lowland areas of the south and east. The north and west is least populated. London is the capital and largest city. Nearly 12 million people live in the London area.

Salford Quays, Manchester

London E

Activities

1 Use map **A** to complete these sentences.
   a) The four countries that make up the UK are ...
   b) The main city in the south east is ....
   c) Two cities in Scotland are ...
   d) The sea off the east coast is ...
   e) The ocean to the west is ...

2 Use chart **F** to measure these distances.
   The first one has been done for you.
   a) Edinburgh to London = **661 km**
   b) Cardiff to Norwich =
   c) Glasgow to Birmingham =
   d) Newcastle to Leeds =
   e) London to Manchester =

Birmingham

166	Cardiff							
470	620	Edinburgh						
470	620	71	Glasgow					
182	373	325	346	Leeds				
192	253	661	639	283	London			
142	295	350	346	64	298	Manchester		
333	523	177	238	148	460	212	Newcastle	
267	422	589	620	283	183	298	425	Norwich

F

3 a) Write a sentence to describe each of the photos **B**, **C**, **D** and **E**. The words below will help you.
   b) Give each description a heading.

B	mountains – moorland – river
C	town – harbour – rugged coast
D	modern buildings – canal – people
E	crowded – buildings – river

Summary

The United Kingdom consists of England, Wales, Scotland and Northern Ireland. The landscape is varied, with mountains in the north and west and lowlands in the south and east. Most people live in the lowland areas.

How developed is the UK?

The UK is one of the wealthiest countries in the world. Its success is due mainly to the growth of industry and trade with other countries. The UK's most important trading partners are countries of the **European Union (EU)**.

Most workers in the UK earn good wages and enjoy a high **standard of living**. They have money to spend on holidays, food and education. They can also afford to buy their own cars and expensive goods like television sets, computers and digital cameras.

All of these things have helped make the UK a **developed country**. A developed country is one that is rich, has many services and a high standard of living.

A — The UK is one of the most developed countries in the world.

We enjoy high standards of living and a good quality of life.

Measures of development in the UK

B

Wealth

There are plenty of jobs here. Most are in well-paid industries like manufacturing and services.

Health

The UK has good health care with well-trained doctors and many high-quality hospitals.

Education

Large amounts of money are spent on education. 99% of UK adults can read and write.

Activities

1 Complete these sentences. The Glossary on pages 166-168 will help you.
   a) Development is …
   b) A developed country is …
   c) Standard of living means …

2 Copy and complete diagram **C** using the following statements.
   ● that have high value …
   ● which makes the country rich.
   ● which exports mainly manufactured goods …
   ● and earn much money …

C

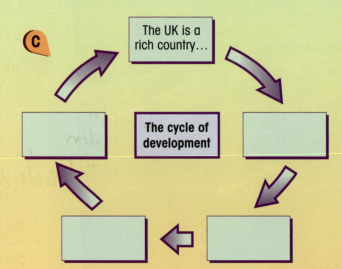

The UK is a rich country…

The cycle of development

Although the UK is a developed country, wealth and high standards of living are not shared equally between everyone. All cities, for example, have some areas that are rich and some that are poor.

Even across the country, there are differences in wealth and standards of living. Look at map **D** which shows average weekly earnings in the UK. Notice the difference between the north and the south.

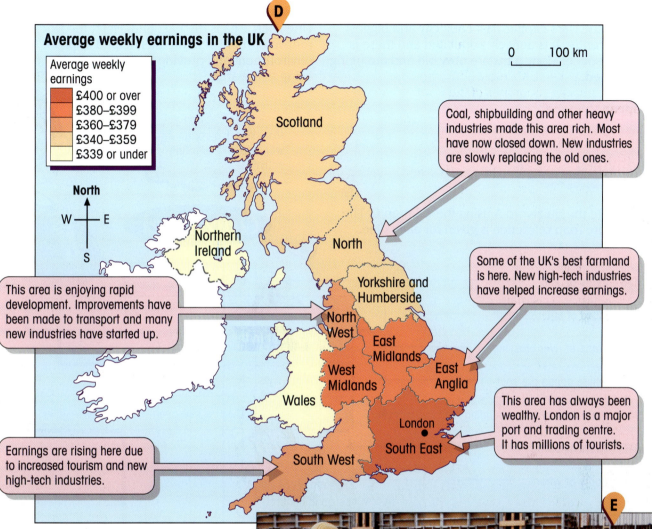

D

Average weekly earnings in the UK

Average weekly earnings

- £400 or over
- £380–£399
- £360–£379
- £340–£359
- £339 or under

0   100 km

North

W ──┼── E

S

Scotland

Northern Ireland

North

Yorkshire and Humberside

North West

East Midlands

West Midlands

East Anglia

Wales

London

South East

South West

Coal, shipbuilding and other heavy industries made this area rich. Most have now closed down. New industries are slowly replacing the old ones.

Some of the UK's best farmland is here. New high-tech industries have helped increase earnings.

This area is enjoying rapid development. Improvements have been made to transport and many new industries have started up.

This area has always been wealthy. London is a major port and trading centre. It has millions of tourists.

Earnings are rising here due to increased tourism and new high-tech industries.

E

Our country is developed but that doesn't mean we're all well off.

3 Look at drawing **B**. Give three reasons why the UK can be described as a developed country.

4 Use map **D** to answer this activity. Complete these sentences.
 a) The average earnings in the north are …
 b) The wealthiest region is …
 c) The regions with the lowest earnings are …
 d) Five things that help make an area rich are …

Summary

The UK is one of the most developed countries in the world. Development is not spread evenly. Some people still have a poor standard of living.

What is London like?

London is the UK's capital, its largest city and biggest industrial centre. It is densely populated and there is little open space. Many parts are now old and are being **redeveloped**.

One such area is the East End. Here, the Docklands redevelopment scheme has helped improve the environment and provide better facilities for people living in the area.

> Mapskills 1 on page 28 will help you with this activity.

Activities

1 Complete the quizword **A** using the OS map **C**. The four-figure map reference is given for each clue.

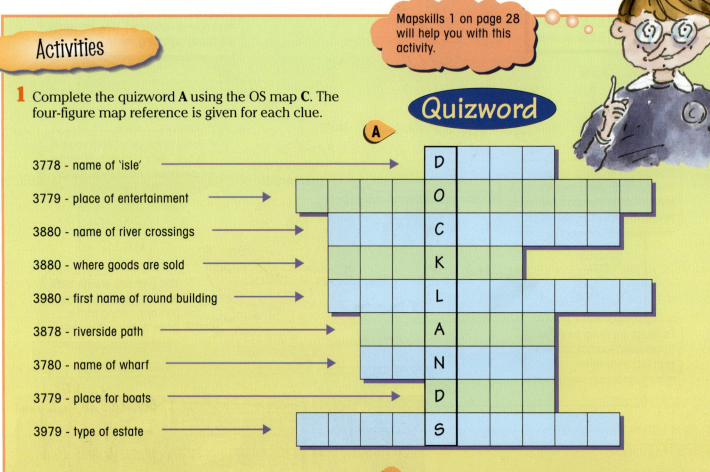

A ◆ Quizword

3778 - name of 'isle' → **D**

3779 - place of entertainment → **O**

3880 - name of river crossings → **C**

3880 - where goods are sold → **K**

3980 - first name of round building → **L**

3878 - riverside path → **A**

3780 - name of wharf → **N**

3779 - place for boats → **D**

3979 - type of estate → **S**

2 Match each of the labels in drawing **B** with a letter from photo **D**.
Answer like this:

A = little *open space*

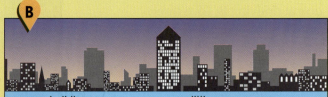

B

- new buildings
- old docks
- River Thames
- Canary Wharf tower
- little open space
- tall buildings
- roads

3 Copy and complete the following sentences using the words from drawing **B**.
- London's East End lies close to the ....
- The area has many .... and ....
- The .... are usually busy and congested.
- The .... are being redeveloped and .... constructed.
- .... is the UK's tallest building.

Summary

London is crowded and always busy. Redevelopment schemes are helping improve conditions in older areas.

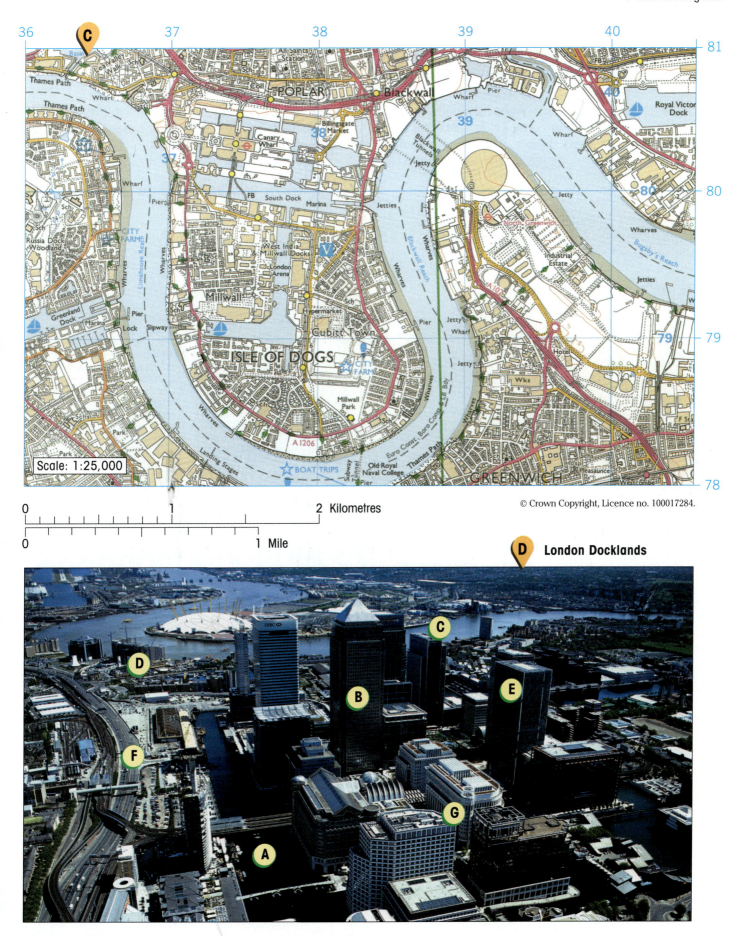

Scale: 1:25,000

0   1   2   Kilometres

0   1   Mile

© Crown Copyright, Licence no. 100017284.

D   **London Docklands**

What is South West England like?

South West England is a mainly **rural** area with few large towns. It has attractive countryside, a spectacular coastline and many pretty villages. The area is popular with tourists. They come mainly for the scenery and the many things that there are to do. Beach activities, sailing and walking are the main activities. Salcombe in south Devon is a typical tourist centre.

Activities

1 Use the OS map **C** for this activity. Name the following features. Answer like this:

Town A =

a) The town at Ⓐ
b) The villages at Ⓑ Ⓒ Ⓓ and Ⓔ
c) The headlands at Ⓕ Ⓖ and Ⓗ
d) The features at Ⓘ and Ⓙ

2 Imagine that you are sailing into Salcombe from point Ⓧ to your mooring at point Ⓨ.
a) List the features from drawing **A** that you would pass on the way. Give them in the correct order.
b) Use the scale-line to measure the length of your journey.

3 Look at the numbered features on photo **D**. Match the numbers to each of these features. The first one has been done for you.

Rolling hills = 5   Jetties =
Salcombe =   Farm =
Church =   Woodland =
Harbour =   Beach =

4 Read description **B**. It is about the Salcombe area shown in photo **D**. Copy and complete the description using the following words.

- Devon   • countryside   • hedgerows
- close   • small boats   • church
- sheltered   • woodland   • wide
- steeply   • town

A

Ferry crossing   Splatcove Point
Biddlehead Point   Batson Creek
Mill Bay   Whitestrand Quay
South Sands   Old Harry Beacon
Lifeboat station   Mudflats
Stink Cove

B

Description of Salcombe

Salcombe is a small .... in south .... It is situated on a .... river estuary and is surrounded by attractive ....

The town is built on .... sloping ground. The buildings are .... together and there is a large .... near the centre. The harbour is .... and full of ....

The area around Salcombe is mainly farmland. The fields are separated by .... and there are many areas of ....

Summary

South West England has fine scenery, attractive villages, an interesting history and plenty of things to do. It is a popular place for tourists.

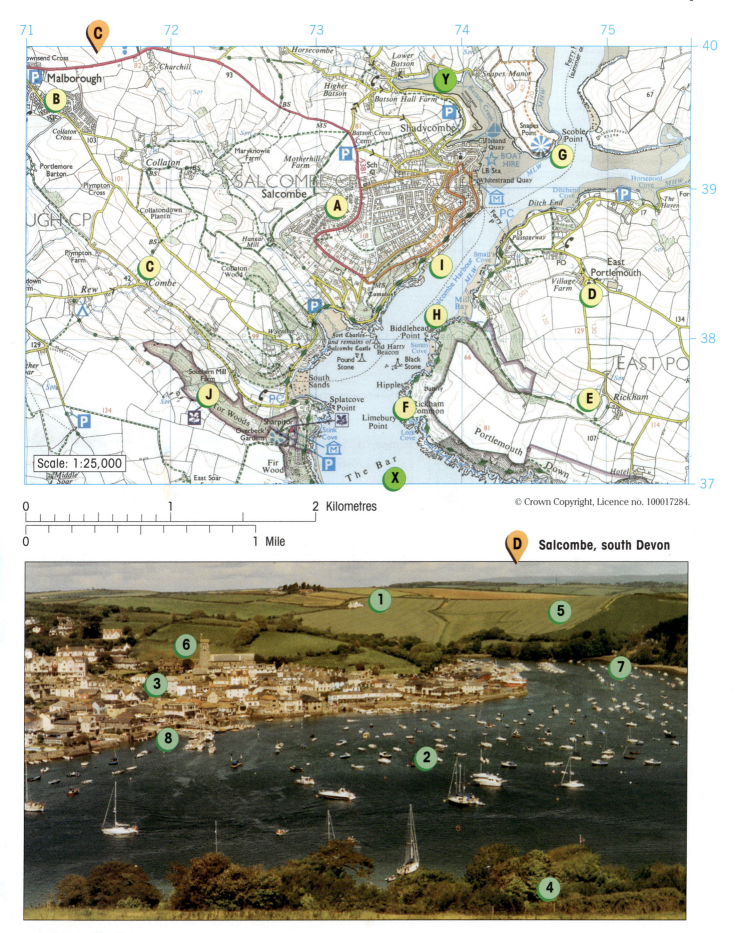

Scale: 1:25,000

0   1   2   Kilometres

0   1 Mile

© Crown Copyright, Licence no. 100017284.

Salcombe, south Devon

How do geographers describe places?

Geography is about people and places and how they affect each other. Look at the photos of the UK on the opposite page. Each one shows a completely different scene. Geography helps us describe these scenes so that we can learn about and understand our world.

So how can we study these places? First we must learn the right words to use. These are called **key words**. For example, one photo shows a pretty **village**. Another shows a **city** and **traffic**. A third is a **mountain** scene and the fourth is a **coast**.

Next we should learn other ways of describing places. These include drawing maps and using facts and figures. Drawing **A** shows three ways in which geographers can describe places.

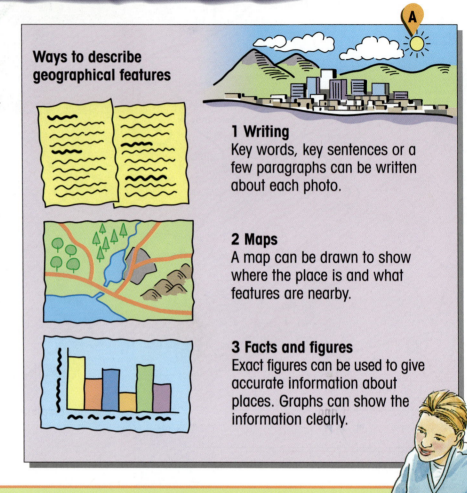

Ways to describe geographical features

1 Writing
Key words, key sentences or a few paragraphs can be written about each photo.

2 Maps
A map can be drawn to show where the place is and what features are nearby.

3 Facts and figures
Exact figures can be used to give accurate information about places. Graphs can show the information clearly.

Activities

1 a) What three ways can be used to describe places?
b) Which method would best show where a place is?
c) Which would give the most exact information?
d) Which could best describe and explain the scene?

2 Look at photos **C**, **D**, **E** and **F**.
List the words from Word Box **B** that may be used to describe each photo. Some words may be used more than once.
Answer like this: **Photo A = village, fields, ...**

3 Write a paragraph about each photo. Include the words from your lists.

B Word Box

stream	fields	buildings
coast	village	shops and offices
traffic	trees	beach
city	moorland	sea
cliffs	people	roads
church	hill	busy
quiet	mountains	snow

Summary

Geography is a subject that studies people and places. Three main ways in which geographers describe places are writing, maps, and facts and figures.

C Naunton, Gloucestershire

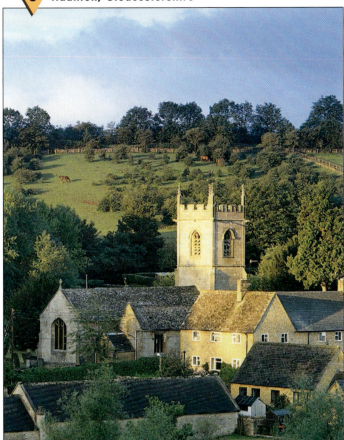

D London

E Glencoe, Scotland

F Slapton Sands, Devon

6 River landforms

What are the main features?

When rain falls to the ground, some of it flows along the surface in rivers or streams.

Rivers wind their way downhill and water drains into them from the surrounding area. Eventually the river may join another river, flow into a lake, or reach the sea.

The River Tees is in northern England. It begins in the Pennine Hills and flows into the North Sea near Middlesbrough. On its way to the sea the river has shaped the land in many different ways. These shapes are called **landforms**.

In this chapter we look at the River Tees and study the landforms it has made.

Activities

1 Look at map **A** and drawing **B**. Match the following places with a **letter** from map **A**. The first one has been done for you.

- Middlesbrough D
- Hartlepool ......
- Darlington ......
- Barnard Castle ......
- North Sea ......
- Pennine Hills ......

2 Look at map **A** and drawing **B**. Match the following features with a **number** from map **A**. The first one has been done for you.

- Mouth 6
- Meander ......
- Tributary ......
- Source ......
- Valley sides ......
- Flood plain ......

3 Match the following beginnings to their correct endings.

Meander	slopes on either side of a river
Waterfall	where a river starts
Valley sides	a northern name for a valley
Source	a flat area that gets covered with water
Dale	a sudden fall of water
Flood plain	a river bend

4 Use drawing **B** to do this activity. Copy and complete the Fact File by finishing the sentences.

River Tees Fact File

- The hills at the source are called ......
- The sea at the mouth is called ......
- The length of the river is ......
- One of the tributaries is called ......
- The main waterfall is called ......
- The large reservoir is called ......

A

(Map A: locations labelled A, B, C, D, E, F; features numbered 1, 2, 3, 4, 5, 6; River Tees; compass showing W, North, S, E; scale 0 — 10 km)

Rivers are found in **valleys**. In northern England where the Tees is located, these valleys are called **dales**. Hence the name Teesdale.

There may be flat ground on either side of the river. This is called the **valley floor**. Settlements are often built here. The slopes on either side of the river are called the **valley sides**.

Most rivers have been flowing for thousands or millions of years. During this time they have worn away their **valleys**, made **waterfalls** and produced **flood plains**.

The Tees is a typical river and shows all these features. Some are shown in the drawing below.

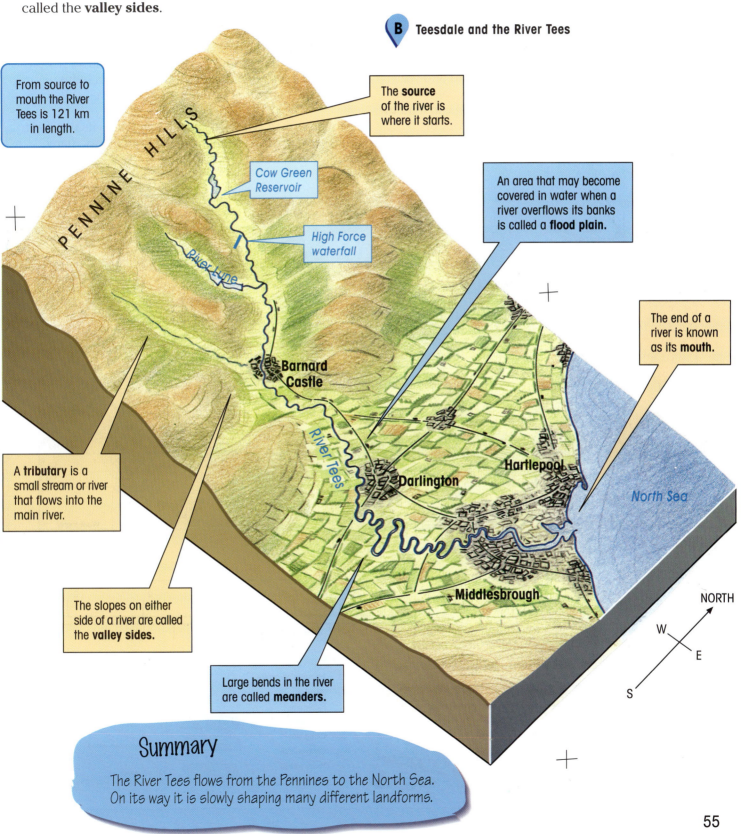

B Teesdale and the River Tees

From source to mouth the River Tees is 121 km in length.

The **source** of the river is where it starts.

Cow Green Reservoir

High Force waterfall

An area that may become covered in water when a river overflows its banks is called a **flood plain**.

The end of a river is known as its **mouth**.

PENNINE HILLS

River Lune

Barnard Castle

River Tees

Hartlepool

Darlington

North Sea

A **tributary** is a small stream or river that flows into the main river.

Middlesbrough

The slopes on either side of a river are called the **valley sides**.

Large bends in the river are called **meanders**.

NORTH
W
E
S

Summary

The River Tees flows from the Pennines to the North Sea. On its way it is slowly shaping many different landforms.

What is Upper Teesdale like?

The Ordnance Survey map **A** below shows part of Upper Teesdale. This is in the Pennines where the River Tees begins. The area is mainly rough moorland with many hill sheep farms. There are a few small villages located on the valley floor.

The weather in Upper Teesdale is often cold and wet. In winter the land may be covered in snow. When the snow melts it causes river levels to rise and can lead to local flooding. The river does most of its work of shaping the land and making landforms when the river is in flood.

Near the top of Upper Teesdale is Cow Green **reservoir**. This is an artificial lake that has been created by building a dam across the river.

The water stored in the reservoir is used in nearby towns like Middlesbrough. The dam also allows people to control the flow of water in the river. This helps reduce the chance of flooding downstream.

Follow the river with your finger as it winds its way from the reservoir down to High Force. Notice how many bends there are on the way.

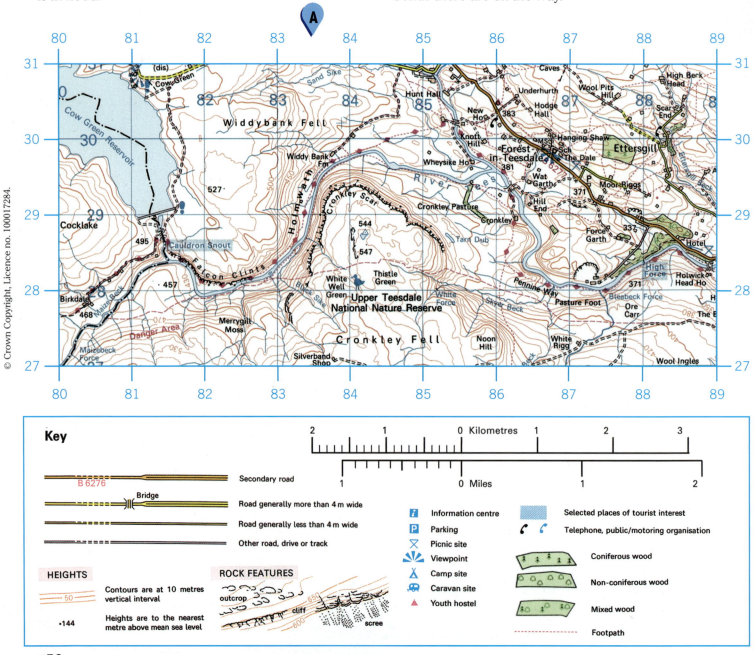

© Crown Copyright, Licence no. 100017284.

B **Upper Teesdale in winter**

The photo **B** is looking west. The small farm is Hill End (8629).

Can you see the bridge in the centre of the photo to the right of Hill End? The River Tees flows under the bridge. It is frozen and covered in snow.

Mapskills 2 – Distance

1. Mark the distance on a piece of paper.

2. Place the paper against the scale.

3. Read off the distance in kilometres. It is **2 km**.

Activities

1. Mapskills 1 on page 28 will help you with this activity. Copy and complete the sentences below using OS map **A** and the key. Choose the grid square from this list. The first one has been done for you.

| 8828 | 8130 | 8629 | 8729 | 8628 |

a) ⊣⊢ is a **bridge** in square **8629**.

b) ⊠ is a .... in square ....

c) ☆ is a .... in square ....

d) .... is a .... in square ....

e) ♠ ♠ is a ....in square ....

2. Look at Mapskills 2 and the OS map. Measure the following distances using the scale. Choose your answers from this list.

① ② ③ ⑤ ⑦

a) Youth hostel (8630) to Hotel (8828) is ...... km.

b) Youth hostel (8630) to Pennine Way (8530) is ...... km.

c) Hill End (8629) to High Force (8828) is ...... km.

d) Dam (8129) to Youth hostel (8630) is ...... km.

e) Dam (8129) to High Force (8828) is ...... km.

3. Follow the river from Cow Green Reservoir to High Force. List the features shown in drawing **C** in the correct order.

C

WIDDY BANK FARM WHEYSIKE HOUSE
BLEABECK FORCE FALCON CLINTS
HILL END HIGH FORCE
CAULDRON SNOUT DAM
RESERVOIR

Summary Ordnance Survey maps show information which can help describe the main features of an area.

What happens on a river bend?

Water flowing in a river channel works very hard and is able to shape the land. If it is flowing quickly it can wear away and move material. If it is flowing slowly it tends to dump material.

Rivers do most of their work when they are in **flood**. This is when they are at their most powerful.

A How a river shapes the land

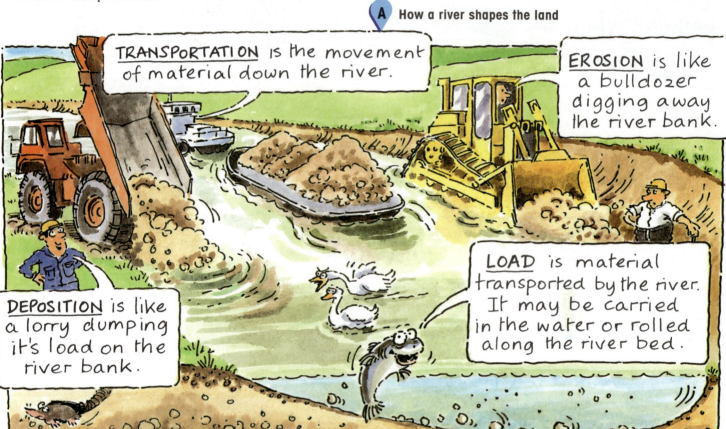

TRANSPORTATION is the movement of material down the river.

EROSION is like a bulldozer digging away the river bank.

DEPOSITION is like a lorry dumping it's load on the river bank.

LOAD is material transported by the river. It may be carried in the water or rolled along the river bed.

Activities

1 The meaning for each of the terms below is in the spiral. Find them by starting at the centre and working outwards. Write out each term with its correct meaning.

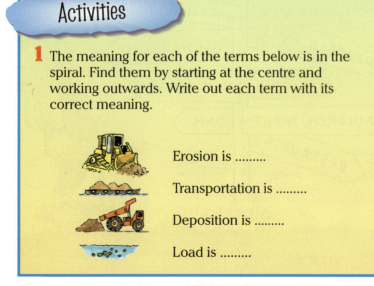

Erosion is ....

Transportation is ....

Deposition is ....

Load is ....

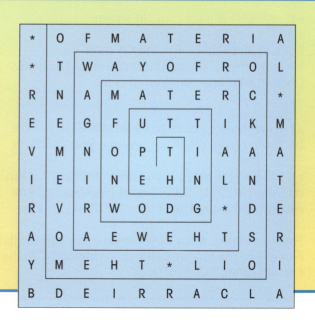

*	O	F	M	A	T	E	R	I	A
*	T	W	A	Y	O	F	R	O	L
R	N	A	M	A	T	E	R	C	*
E	E	G	F	U	T	T	I	K	M
V	M	N	O	P	T	I	A	A	A
I	E	I	N	E	H	N	L	N	T
R	V	R	W	O	D	G	*	D	E
A	O	A	E	W	E	H	T	S	R
Y	M	E	H	T	*	L	I	O	I
B	D	E	I	R	R	A	C	L	A

As we have seen, a river's course is seldom straight. Photo **B** below shows a bend or meander in Upper Teesdale. It is in grid square 8429 on page 56.

As the water flows round the bend it moves fastest on the outside. This causes erosion. On the inside of the bend, the water flows more slowly. This causes deposition and a build-up of material.

B Features of a river bend in Upper Teesdale

Inside of bend
- Slowest flow
- Deposition
- Gentle slope
- Shallow water

Outside of bend
- Fastest flow
- Erosion
- River cliff
- Deep water

2 Look at the two lists below. They describe what happens on a river bend, but the information is in the wrong order. Write out each list in the correct order.

On the **inside** of the bend …
- this builds up material
- the water flows slowest
- and makes the channel shallow
- so deposition happens

On the **outside** of a bend …
- and deepens the channel
- so erosion happens
- this wears away the banks
- the river flows fastest

3 The river bend above is in grid square 8429 on map **A** on page 56. The farm in the background is about 1 km west of the bend. Find it on the map.
a) Name the farm and give its grid reference.
b) What is the height of the hill behind the farm?

Summary

Rivers usually have many bends. The outside of a bend is worn away by erosion. The inside is built up by deposition.

What causes waterfalls?

Waterfalls are the most spectacular of river landforms. Some are almost 1,000 metres high. Others are much smaller. Whatever their size they are almost all attractive and impressive landform features.

Waterfalls usually occur when rivers flow over different types of rock. Often, the difference in the rock is that one is hard and one is soft. When this happens, the soft rock wears away faster than the hard rock.

After hundreds or thousands of years this will cause a step to develop. The water plunges down the step as a waterfall.

As time goes by, the water cuts away rock behind the waterfall. This causes the falls to move back up the valley. When this happens, it leaves a steep-sided **gorge**.

A A section through a waterfall

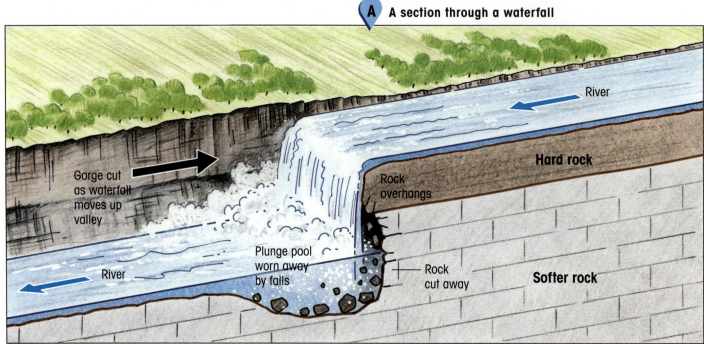

B How a waterfall wears away

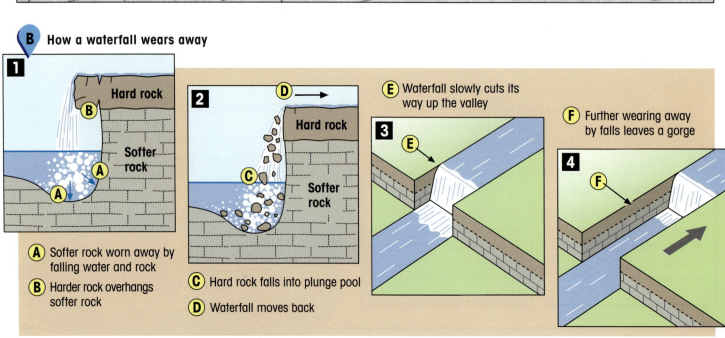

Ⓐ Softer rock worn away by falling water and rock

Ⓑ Harder rock overhangs softer rock

Ⓒ Hard rock falls into plunge pool

Ⓓ Waterfall moves back

Ⓔ Waterfall slowly cuts its way up the valley

Ⓕ Further wearing away by falls leaves a gorge

C High Force waterfall on the River Tees

Labels on photo: Hard whinstone, E, D, A, F, B, C, Soft limestone

One of Britain's best-known waterfalls is High Force in Upper Teesdale. The falls are some 20 metres high. When the river is in flood, this is one of the finest sights in England.

At High Force, hard rock lies on top of soft rock. The force of the falling water wears away the soft rock. Eventually the hard rock above collapses and the waterfall moves back.

The gorge below High Force is over 700 metres in length. In many years' time it will be even longer.

D

HIGH FORCE

gorge formed

waterfall moves back

water plunges over falls

hard rock undercut

hard rock collapses

soft rock worn away

RANGER

Activities

1 Copy and complete the Fact File below.

Fact File: High Force

- Location – where is it?
- Grid reference – page 24
- Height – in metres
- Type of rock – on top
- Type of rock – underneath
- Length of gorge – in metres

2 Look at photo **C** above and match the letters with the words below.
Answer like this: Ⓐ = Waterfall

Softer rock undercut

Plunge pool

Hard rock overhangs

Waterfall

Gorge

River

3 The phrases in drawing **D** above show how a waterfall may be worn away. Put them into the correct order. Number them 1, 2, 3, 4, 5 and 6.

Summary

Waterfalls occur when water wears away soft rock more quickly than hard rock. As a waterfall erodes back, a gorge may be formed.

What is the flooding problem?

A river can only carry a certain amount of water. When it becomes too full it will overflow and cover the surrounding area. This is called a **flood**. The area flooded is called the **floodplain**.

There are many different causes of flooding. The most common is heavy rain over a long period of time. Drawing **A** shows some of the main reasons why a river might flood. There is more information about flooding on pages 14 and 15.

A When is flooding most likely to happen?

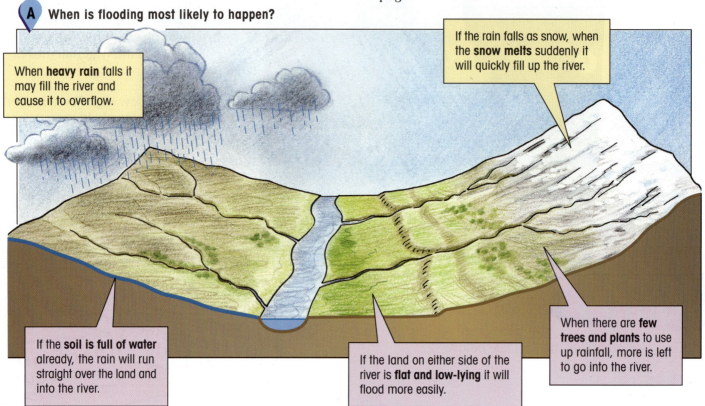

If the rain falls as snow, when the **snow melts** suddenly it will quickly fill up the river.

When **heavy rain** falls it may fill the river and cause it to overflow.

If the **soil is full of water** already, the rain will run straight over the land and into the river.

If the land on either side of the river is **flat and low-lying** it will flood more easily.

When there are **few trees and plants** to use up rainfall, more is left to go into the river.

Floods cause damage to property and problems for people living in the area.

There is therefore a need to try to stop flooding or at least to reduce the problem as much as possible.

One way of reducing the chance of a flood is to build a dam to control the river flow. Other methods are shown in diagram **B**.

B How might flooding be reduced?

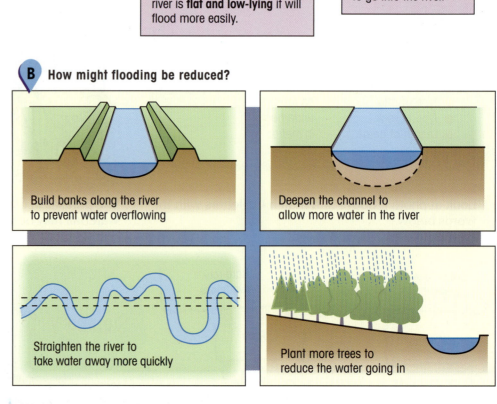

Build banks along the river to prevent water overflowing

Deepen the channel to allow more water in the river

Straighten the river to take water away more quickly

Plant more trees to reduce the water going in

Like most rivers, the River Tees is liable to flood. In recent times, flooding of the Tees has been less of a problem. This is because the dam at Cow Green Reservoir has helped control the river's flow. Flooding does still happen, though.

Map **C** below shows part of the river where a flood protection scheme has been considered. The plan would be to straighten the river, strengthen the banks and deepen the channel.

A plan like this may not satisfy everyone.

C

Farm

220

210

Pub

200

Activities centre

Caravan park

Old mill

210

Gravel works

Houses

200

210 Rescue services

Pony trekking

● Areas below 200 metres may be flooded

Key

Old course

New course

—200— Height

Road

0   1 km

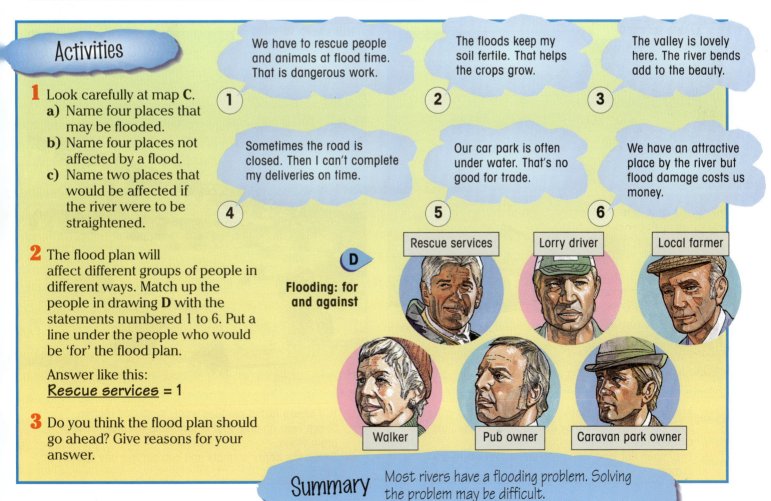

Activities

We have to rescue people and animals at flood time. That is dangerous work. **1**

The floods keep my soil fertile. That helps the crops grow. **2**

The valley is lovely here. The river bends add to the beauty. **3**

1 Look carefully at map **C**.
  a) Name four places that may be flooded.
  b) Name four places not affected by a flood.
  c) Name two places that would be affected if the river were to be straightened.

Sometimes the road is closed. Then I can't complete my deliveries on time. **4**

Our car park is often under water. That's no good for trade. **5**

We have an attractive place by the river but flood damage costs us money. **6**

Rescue services

Lorry driver

Local farmer

2 The flood plan will affect different groups of people in different ways. Match up the people in drawing **D** with the statements numbered 1 to 6. Put a line under the people who would be 'for' the flood plan.

D

Flooding: for and against

Answer like this:
Rescue services = 1

Walker

Pub owner

Caravan park owner

3 Do you think the flood plan should go ahead? Give reasons for your answer.

Summary Most rivers have a flooding problem. Solving the problem may be difficult.

What types of farming are there in Britain?

Most people have to **work** for a living. Another word for the work that they do is **industry**. There are many different types of work and industry. Together they are called **economic activities**.

One group of economic activities is called **primary industry**. Primary industry is when people collect **natural resources**. These natural resources are sometimes called **raw materials**. Farming is an example of a primary industry.

Farming, or **agriculture**, is the way that people produce food by growing crops and raising animals. The four main types of farming in Britain are shown below.

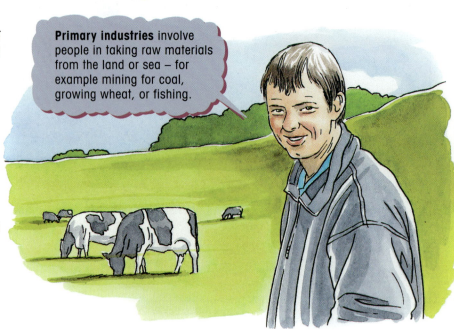

Primary industries involve people in taking raw materials from the land or sea – for example mining for coal, growing wheat, or fishing.

A

Arable farming

- **Arable farms** grow crops. They include cereal crops such as wheat and barley and vegetables like potatoes and carrots.
- They need flat land with good soil and a warm dry climate.

Hill sheep farming

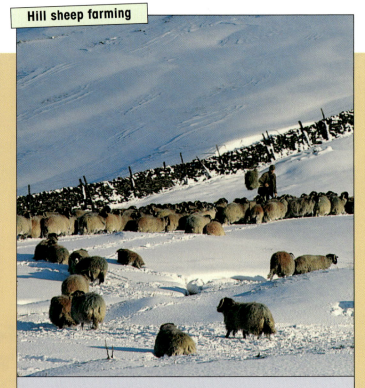

- **Hill sheep farms** produce wool, lamb and mutton. Sheep feed on land that is too steep to raise cattle or grow crops.
- Sheep are hardy animals and can survive any climate in Britain.

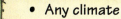

1 Complete the following sentences. The Glossary on pages 166 to 168 will help you.
   a) Primary industries are ...
   b) Natural resources are ...
   c) Raw materials are ...
   d) Farming is ...

2 Make a larger copy of table **B**. Put the statements from drawing **C** into the correct columns. Some may be used more than once.

B

Farming type	Description	Needs
Arable		
Hill sheep		
Cattle		
Mixed		

C

- Any climate
- Flat or gently sloping land
- Produce wool, lamb and mutton
- Good soil
- Warm, dry climate
- Raise animals and grow crops
- Produce milk or beef
- Most types of land
- Grow crops
- Warm, moist climate
- Flat land

Summary

The main types of farming in Britain are arable, hill sheep, cattle and mixed. The type of farming that is best for an area depends on many different factors.

Cattle farming

- **Cattle farms** raise cows to produce milk or beef. Raising cows for milk is called **dairy farming**.
- Cows need land that is not too steep, and a warm, moist climate for grass to grow well.

Mixed farming

- **Mixed farms** grow crops and raise livestock.
- They need fairly good soil and a climate that is neither too wet nor too dry. Flat or gently sloping is good for the cattle and makes it easy to move modern machinery.

What is the pattern of farming in Britain?

The type of farming that is most suited to an area depends on several different factors. These include **physical factors** such as:

- the shape and height of the land
- the type, quality and depth of the soils
- the climate, including sunshine, rainfall and temperature.

These factors are not the same everywhere but vary from place to place. This helps explain why there are differences in farming types across the country.

An accurate map showing where the main farming types are found in Britain would be very complicated. Map **A** is a simplified map which is easy to draw and to understand. It shows how the pattern of farming in Britain changes from the north and west to the south and east.

Simplified map to show the pattern of farming in Britain

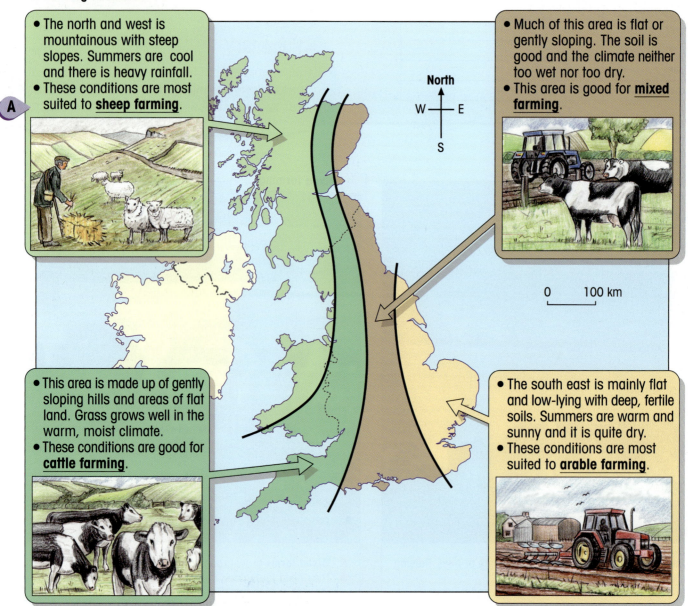

A

- The north and west is mountainous with steep slopes. Summers are cool and there is heavy rainfall.
- These conditions are most suited to **sheep farming**.

- Much of this area is flat or gently sloping. The soil is good and the climate neither too wet nor too dry.
- This area is good for **mixed farming**.

- This area is made up of gently sloping hills and areas of flat land. Grass grows well in the warm, moist climate.
- These conditions are good for **cattle farming**.

- The south east is mainly flat and low-lying with deep, fertile soils. Summers are warm and sunny and it is quite dry.
- These conditions are most suited to **arable farming**.

North

W — E

S

0   100 km

Market gardens are small farms that grow high-value crops such as fruit, vegetables and flowers. They use modern methods and the latest high-tech machinery and equipment.

The location of market gardens depends mainly on **human factors** rather than physical factors. This is because in most market gardens, soils and climate are artificially controlled inside huge greenhouses.

The most important location factor is to be near large towns and cities or close to motorways. This is so that the fruit, vegetables and flowers will be fresh when they reach the shops. They can then attract the highest prices and make most money for the farmer.

Here are some things grown on a market garden:

B A market garden greenhouse

Activities

1 Use map **A** to do this activity. Copy and complete these sentences to describe the pattern of farming in Britain.
   a) The north and west is mainly .... farming.
   b) The south west is good for .... farming.
   c) Central England is mainly .... farming.
   d) The east is more suited to .... farming.

2 Copy and complete these sentences.
   a) A market garden is ...
   b) Market gardens are located close to ... because ...

3 Match the numbers on map **C** with the following farming types. Some may be used more than once. Map **A** will help you.
   Answer like this: **1 = Cattle farming**

● Sheep	● Cattle	● Mixed
● Arable	● Market gardening	

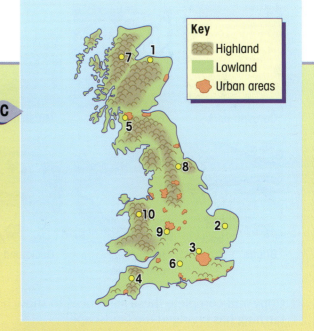

C

Key
Highland
Lowland
Urban areas

Summary

The pattern of farming in Britain depends mainly on physical factors. Market gardens need to be near to large urban areas.

How has farming changed the landscape?

Most of Britain was once covered in forest and marshland. As farming developed, the forests were cleared and marshes were drained. Later, hedges were planted and stone walls built to make fields. This farming landscape lasted for many hundreds of years.

In recent times, there have been further changes to the landscape. Hedgerows and woodlands have now been cleared and wetlands drained. Field sizes have been increased and tourist developments have begun to appear. Some of these changes can be seen in the drawings on page 69.

Activities

1 Find at least ten differences between the landscape in the 1940s and the same area in the 2000s.

2 Match the features below with the correct grid squares.
Answer like this: **A2 is farm buildings.**

A2 is ....   D2 is ....   B5 is ....

F4 is ....   F10 is ....   A3 is ....

Caravan park

Farm buildings

Marshland

Bridge

Hedgerows and fences

Duckpond

3 Copy and complete these sentences to show how farming has changed the landscape.
The first one has been done for you.
a) Small fields (E3) made into **large fields** (E8)
b) Farmland (F5) changed to ...... (F10)
c) Marshland (B5) changed to ...... (B10)
d) Hedges (C4) replaced by ...... (C9)
e) Woodland (F3) cleared for ...... (F8)

4 Give three other changes in the area. Answer in the same way as you did for activity 3.

5 Give the grid square for the following. The first one has been done for you.
a) Larger buildings increase storage **H7**
b) Home for wildlife lost as hedges cut down ...
c) Natural vegetation lost as marshland drained ...
d) Traffic danger increased by new caravan park ...
e) Farming improved by larger fields ...

6 The farmer below lives in grid square E9. Copy and complete the speech bubble to show how the farm has changed since the 1940s.

**The main change is ...
Another important change is ...
Other changes include ...**

Local farmer

Summary

The appearance of much of Britain's landscape is a result of farming. As farming changes, then so does the landscape.

SPOT THE DIFFERENCE!

What is the hedgerow problem?

Hedges have been part of the landscape for hundreds of years. They act as field boundaries and stop animals from wandering. Most people consider them to be an attractive feature of the countryside. They are also important to the **environment**.

As drawing **A** shows, hedges are home to a great variety of wildlife. They also provide food and shelter. Without hedges, many birds, insects, animals and plants would struggle to survive.

Sadly, hedgerows are gradually disappearing from our countryside. In the last fifty years almost half of the UK's hedges have been lost. Most have been removed by farmers.

Farmers do care about the countryside, but hedges take up land and are expensive to look after. As farming methods change, it is often easier for the farmer to remove hedges.

Conservationists are people who care for and look after the environment. They believe that the countryside needs to be protected.

Farmers and **conservationists** often disagree about this. Conservationists want to protect **natural habitats** and keep the countryside as it is. Farmers argue that they need to produce food and make a living.

A

A typical hedgerow

Moths, spiders, butterflies and ladybirds

Blackbird

Chaffinch

Hawthorn

Honeysuckle

Foxglove

Yellowhammer

Rabbit

Poppy

Ivy

Cowslip

Weasel

Primrose

Hedgehog

Partridge

Voles and mice

Squirrel

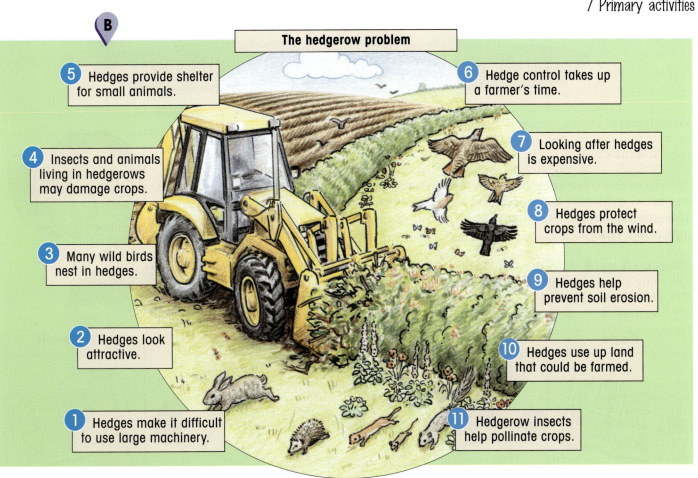

The hedgerow problem

5 Hedges provide shelter for small animals.

6 Hedge control takes up a farmer's time.

4 Insects and animals living in hedgerows may damage crops.

7 Looking after hedges is expensive.

8 Hedges protect crops from the wind.

3 Many wild birds nest in hedges.

9 Hedges help prevent soil erosion.

2 Hedges look attractive.

10 Hedges use up land that could be farmed.

1 Hedges make it difficult to use large machinery.

11 Hedgerow insects help pollinate crops.

B

Activities

1 List the wildlife that may be found in a hedgerow. Sort them under the headings:
- Birds   - Insects   - Animals   - Plants.

2 Make a copy of table **C**. Sort the statements from drawing **B** into the correct columns.
You need only write the number. The first one has been done for you.

C

Hedgerows	
Advantages	Disadvantages
	1

3 Show the views of the people in drawing **D** by completing the speech bubbles. Drawing **B** and your answer to activity 2 will help you.

4 Decide whether you are for or against hedgerows. Write a report on the problem, using the writing frame on page 43.

D

We prefer to keep hedgerows because ...... and ......

I want to get rid of hedgerows because ...... and ......

Conservationists

Local farmer

Summary

Hedgerows are an attractive and important feature of the landscape. Farmers and conservationists disagree about their removal.

What are key words and key sentences?

Written text in books, newspapers and magazines can be long and complicated. This can make it difficult to read and understand.

To help us use these sources of information we must learn how to identify **key words** and **key sentences**. This can help us simplify the text and learn about the topic more easily.

Drawings **A** and **B** show how we can do this by following four easy steps. The examples used are two different types of farming.

> **Key words** and **key sentences** are the most important and useful pieces of information in a paragraph.

A

Read	Identify	Write	Research

B

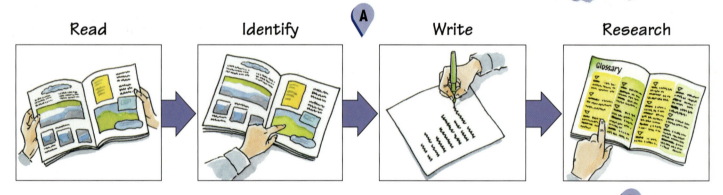

1. **Read** each paragraph very carefully. There is usually one important piece of information in each sentence.

2. **Identify** the key words and key sentences. These may include technical terms that are special to geography.

3. **Write down** the key words and key sentences as a list.

4. **Research** and **write down** the meaning of each key word and key sentence that you are not sure about. You could ask your teacher or use a textbook or glossary for this.

Roseberry Farm is located close to Cambridge in South East England. It is a large and efficient farm and uses modern equipment and the latest high-tech methods.

The land on the farm is flat or gently sloping and the soil is deep and rich in nutrients. The area around Cambridge is one of the driest parts of Britain. Much of the rain falls in the growing season when it is most needed. Summers are generally warm with plenty of sunshine to ripen crops.

These physical factors provide ideal conditions for arable farming. The flat land makes it easy to use heavy machinery and the climate and soils are suited to growing crops. Wheat, potatoes, peas and sugar beet are grown at Roseberry Farm. These are sold to large companies such as Bird's Eye and Tesco.

C

Stancombe Farm is in Devon, in South West England. The farm is quite small with just twelve fields surrounded by high hedgerows. There are three large barns and a stone-built farmhouse.

This part of Devon has a landscape of gently sloping hills and flat valley floors. The soil is fertile and well drained. The climate of the area is warm and moist. Summers are sunny with temperatures usually over 20°C. Winters are mild and there are rarely any frosts.

These physical factors are ideal for dairy farming. The relief is suited to raising cattle whilst the soils and climate are good for growing grass. The Kingsley family, who own and run the property, keep cattle for milk and also make dairy products including cheese and yoghurt.

Activities

1 Look at the information in **B**.
 a) Read about Roseberry Farm.
 b) Identify the key words and key sentences. They are underlined in green.
 c) Write out the key words and key sentences.
 d) Research the meaning of any words or technical terms that you don't know. Write them out.

2 Make a copy of the farm fact file **D**. Complete it for Roseberry Farm using key words and key questions from drawing **B**. Not all the key words and key questions will be used.

3 Look at drawing **C** and repeat activities 1 and 2 for Stancombe Farm. You will need to choose your own key words and key sentences this time.

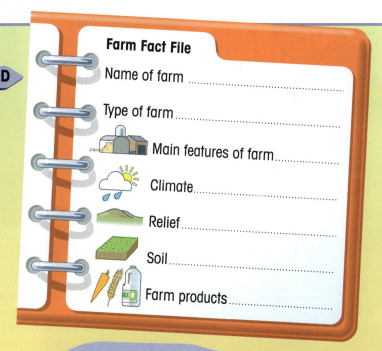

D

Farm Fact File

Name of farm ....

Type of farm ....

Main features of farm ....

Climate ....

Relief ....

Soil ....

Farm products ....

Summary

The most important pieces of information in written text are known as key words and key sentences.

What types of work are there?

Most people have to **work** to provide the things they need in life. Another word for the work they do is **industry**.

There are many different types of work and industry. Together they are called **economic activities**. **Economic** means money and wealth.

The work people do can be divided into three main types. These are **primary**, **secondary** and **tertiary**. They are explained below.

 A

Primary industries involve people in collecting the Earth's **natural resources**. Farming and mining are examples of primary jobs. They take food and coal from the ground.

B

Secondary industries employ people to make things. These are usually made from raw materials. Most secondary jobs are in factories. **Manufacturing** is another name for this industry.

C

Tertiary industries provide a service. They give help to others. No goods are made in this industry. Teaching and nursing are examples of tertiary jobs.

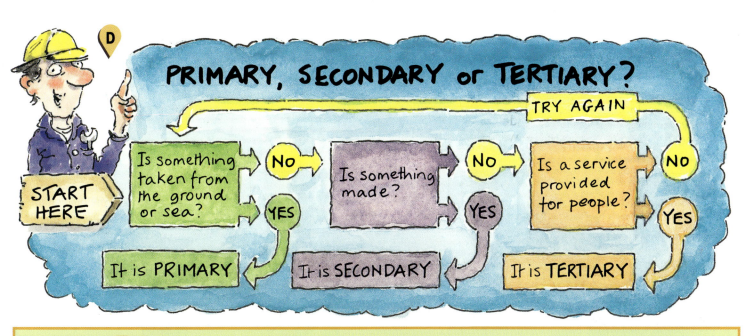

PRIMARY, SECONDARY or TERTIARY?

TRY AGAIN

START HERE → Is something taken from the ground or sea? — **NO** → Is something made? — **NO** → Is a service provided for people? — **NO** → *(TRY AGAIN)*

- YES → It is PRIMARY
- YES → It is SECONDARY
- YES → It is TERTIARY

Activities

1 Use diagram **D** above to help you answer this activity. Copy table **E**. Put the jobs and companies shown in **F**, into the correct columns.

2 What job would you like to do when you leave school? Is it primary, secondary or tertiary? Add it to your table.

3 Ask five other people in the class what they want to do. Add those jobs to your table.

E

Primary	Secondary	Tertiary

F

IBM

Alfred Biggs Ltd — Building Contractors

Stockland Golf and Country Club

Stephens and Son Ltd — *fine glassware*

Peter Barratt's GARDEN CENTRES

*S*ewing machine operator — Skilled work at reasonable prices

R. Wallis **Geography teacher**

DOWNSIDE COLLIERY — Experts in coal mining

VANDAM Car manufacturers

Frederick Lambert *Master bricklayer*

Fleetwood Fisheries

Summary

Work may be divided into three main groups. These are primary, secondary and tertiary.

75

What is the car industry?

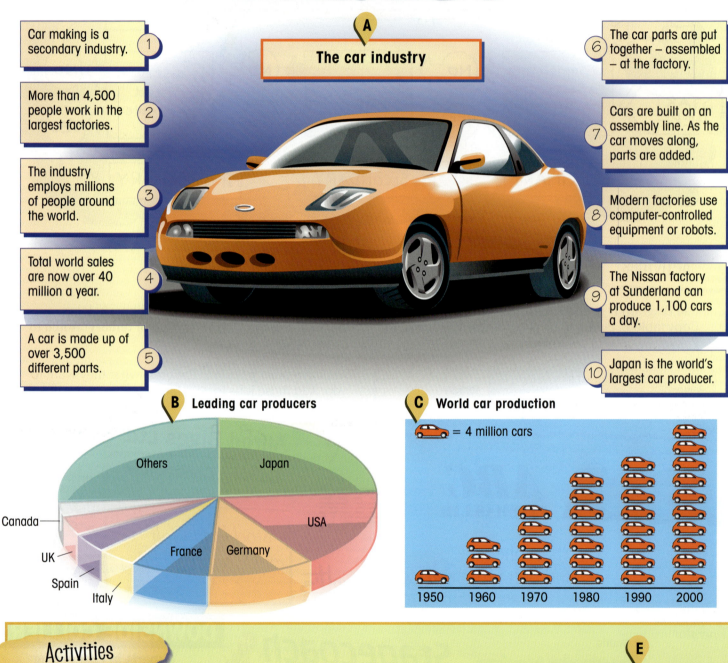

A The car industry

1 Car making is a secondary industry.

2 More than 4,500 people work in the largest factories.

3 The industry employs millions of people around the world.

4 Total world sales are now over 40 million a year.

5 A car is made up of over 3,500 different parts.

6 The car parts are put together – assembled – at the factory.

7 Cars are built on an assembly line. As the car moves along, parts are added.

8 Modern factories use computer-controlled equipment or robots.

9 The Nissan factory at Sunderland can produce 1,100 cars a day.

10 Japan is the world's largest car producer.

B Leading car producers

Others, Japan, USA, Germany, France, Italy, Spain, UK, Canada

C World car production

= 4 million cars

1950 1960 1970 1980 1990 2000

Activities

1 a) Make a copy of table **D** below.
b) Sort the facts from diagram **A** above into the correct columns. You need only give the number for each one.

2 Look at graph **B**. List the world's four largest car producers.

3 Look at graph **C**. Copy and complete table **E**.

D

The car industry	
World facts	Factory facts

E

World car production	
Year	Cars in millions
1950	
1960	
1970	
1980	
1990	
2000	

The UK car industry employs over 200,000 people. In 2000 it made £7.4 billion from selling cars to other countries. These are called **exports**. They are good for Britain's **trade**.

Most of the world's car manufacturers now have factories in Britain. As map **F** shows, they are located in three main areas. These are:
1 the South-east near to London
2 the Midlands around Birmingham
3 the North-west close to Liverpool.

All of the factories are located near to large towns. This is so that workers from the towns may be employed in the factory. They may also buy many of the finished cars.

In recent years some Japanese firms have opened factories in Britain. This has helped increase the number of cars produced.

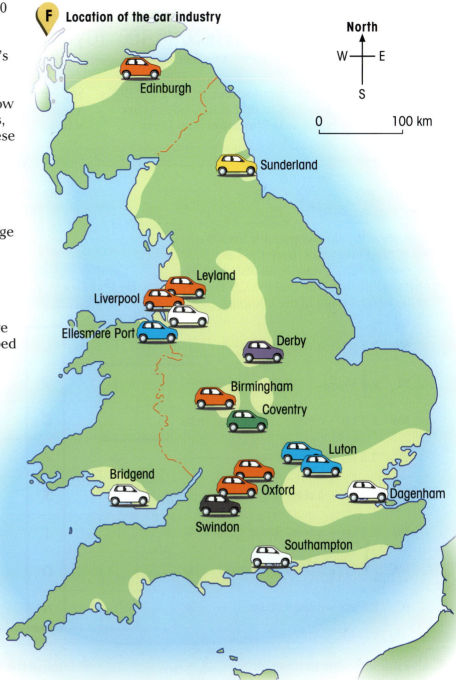

F Location of the car industry

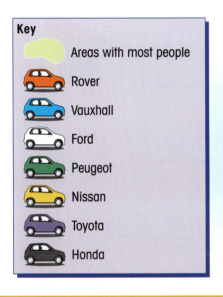

Key

Areas with most people

Rover

Vauxhall

Ford

Peugeot

Nissan

Toyota

Honda

4 Look at map **F**. Name the car company at each of these locations. The first one has been done for you.

Edinburgh – *Rover*
Liverpool –
Luton –
Dagenham –
Coventry –
Sunderland –
Derby –
Swindon –

5 Of the six statements given below, four are correct. Write out the correct ones.
● Most car companies are located in the north.
● Most car companies are located in three main areas.
● Car companies need to be in places where there are many people.
● Car companies prefer to be in the countryside.
● The Midlands is an important car-producing area.
● Japanese companies have helped increase car sales.

Summary

Car making is an important secondary industry. Car companies are located close to large towns.

Where is the Toyota factory?

Toyota is a Japanese car manufacturer. In the early 1990s it decided to build a factory in Britain to produce cars. The place Toyota chose was Burnaston near Derby.

You can see the location of the factory on the OS map. It is in grid squares 2830 and 2930. The town of Derby is just off the map to the north-east.

Activities

Mapskills 1 (page 28) and Mapskills 2 (page 56) will help you with these activities.

1 Complete the quizword using the OS map. Start every clue from the Car Factory at 2830. Measure all distances in a straight line. Imagine that the Car Factory is the central point of the compass.

Quizword

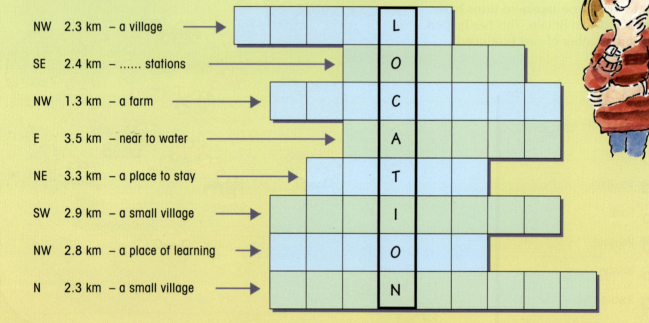

NW	2.3 km	– a village	→					**L**	
SE	2.4 km	– ...... stations	→					**O**	
NW	1.3 km	– a farm	→					**C**	
E	3.5 km	– near to water	→					**A**	
NE	3.3 km	– a place to stay	→					**T**	
SW	2.9 km	– a small village	→					**I**	
NW	2.8 km	– a place of learning	→					**O**	
N	2.3 km	– a small village	→					**N**	

2 Use the scale-line to measure the size of the Car Factory. Answer like this.

Width (w) = ... km
Length (l) = ... km

3 Look at the OS map opposite and the sketch map below it. Name the features at ⓐ ⓑ ⓒ ⓓ and ⓔ.

Answer like this:
ⓐ = railway line

4 Look at the list below. It gives some reasons why Toyota chose this area for their car factory. Match a letter ⓕ ⓖ ⓗ ⓘ ⓙ ⓚ or ⓛ with each reason. The first one has been done to help you.

- Room for expansion (get larger) = ⓕ
- Pleasant villages nearby =
- Near to trunk road =
- Power stations =
- Near to railway station =
- Nearby leisure facilities =
- Large area of flat ground =

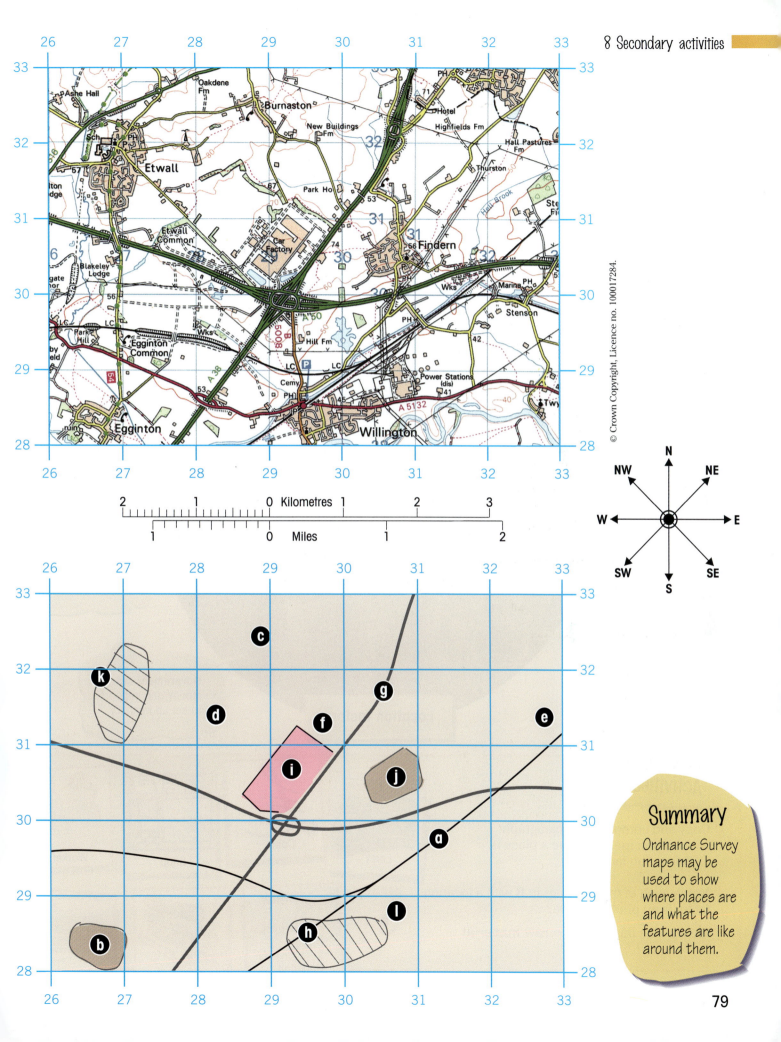

© Crown Copyright, Licence no. 100017284.

Summary

Ordnance Survey maps may be used to show where places are and what the features are like around them.

How did Toyota choose the site for their factory?

If a business is to be successful it must be **located** in the right place. A shop, for example, should have lots of customers living nearby. A frozen food factory must be close to its food supply so that the food can be frozen while it is still fresh. A farm needs plenty of land.

Decisions about where to open a shop, build a factory or start a farm are carefully made. The many different things to consider when making the choice are called **location factors**. Seven of these are shown in figure **A** below.

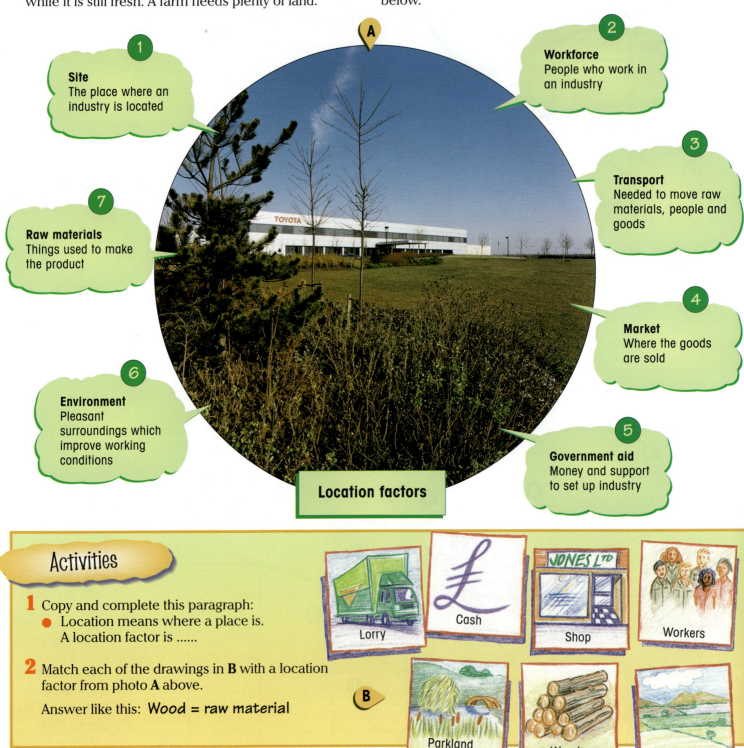

A

1 Site
The place where an industry is located

2 Workforce
People who work in an industry

3 Transport
Needed to move raw materials, people and goods

4 Market
Where the goods are sold

5 Government aid
Money and support to set up industry

6 Environment
Pleasant surroundings which improve working conditions

7 Raw materials
Things used to make the product

Location factors

Activities

1 Copy and complete this paragraph:
  ● Location means where a place is.
    A location factor is ......

2 Match each of the drawings in **B** with a location factor from photo **A** above.

  Answer like this: *Wood = raw material*

B

Lorry

Cash

JONES LTD — Shop

Workers

Parkland

Wood

Flat land

In the late 1980s, Toyota decided that they wanted to build a car factory in Britain. Choosing the best site took a long time and needed careful planning.

First they listed the location factors that were important to them. Then they looked at several possible sites across Europe. Finally they decided on Burnaston near Derby. The first car was produced there in December 1992.

So what was it about Burnaston that made it the best location? Some of the reasons are given in figure **C** below.

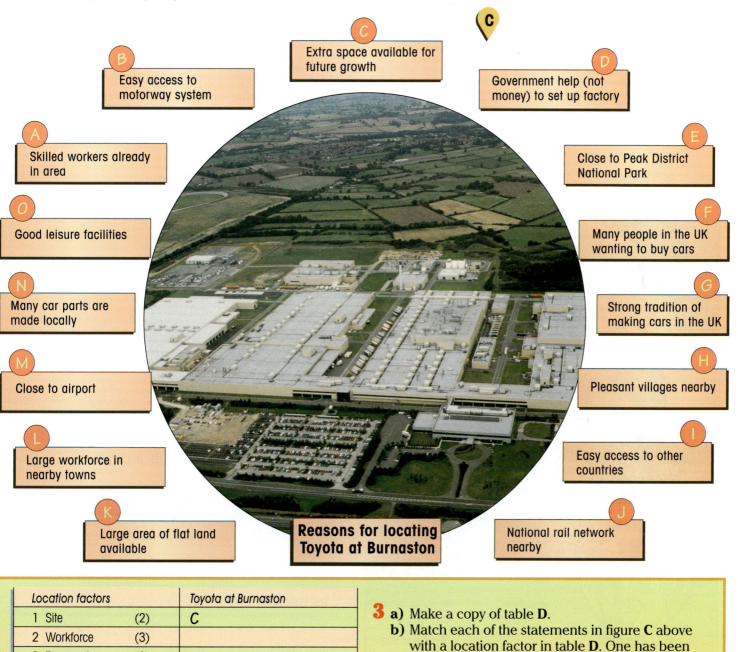

C

B Easy access to motorway system

C Extra space available for future growth

D Government help (not money) to set up factory

A Skilled workers already in area

E Close to Peak District National Park

O Good leisure facilities

F Many people in the UK wanting to buy cars

N Many car parts are made locally

G Strong tradition of making cars in the UK

M Close to airport

H Pleasant villages nearby

L Large workforce in nearby towns

I Easy access to other countries

K Large area of flat land available

Reasons for locating Toyota at Burnaston

J National rail network nearby

Location factors		Toyota at Burnaston
1 Site	(2)	C
2 Workforce	(3)	
3 Transport	(3)	
4 Market	(2)	
5 Government help	(1)	
6 Environment	(3)	
7 Raw materials	(1)	

D

The figures in brackets ( ) show how many of the statements in photo **C** relate to each factor.

3 a) Make a copy of table **D**.
b) Match each of the statements in figure **C** above with a location factor in table **D**. One has been done for you.

Summary

Location factors are used to help choose the best site for an industry. Burnaston near Derby is an ideal location for the Toyota car factory.

Industrial change: good or bad?

New industry can very easily change an area. It may bring many benefits but it can also cause problems.

When plans for the Toyota factory were first made public, most people in the Derby area welcomed the proposals. They were pleased about the new jobs that it would bring. They thought the development might attract other industries to the area. And they liked the idea of a new modern industry locating near to them.

Others were not quite so sure. They wondered about the extra noise and pollution that a huge factory would bring. They were also concerned about the loss of open countryside.

What do you think about industrial developments like this? Do you think they are good, or do you think they are bad? Look at the cartoons **C** opposite, which show some people's views.

Activities

Shop owner

School leaver

Bird watcher

Transporter driver

- Work in pairs or a small group for these activities. This will help you share each other's views and ideas.

- You will need to use the cartoons in **C** opposite to answer each activity.

1 a) Which cartoons are good news?
b) Which cartoons are bad news?

Answer like this: 1 = *good*

2 Some of the people shown in **A** may be **for** the Toyota factory and some **against** it. Copy and complete table **B** to show their views.

	For or *against*	Reason
The shop owner		
The school leaver		
The bird watcher		
The transporter driver		

3 Complete the sentences below.
- In my view, the Toyota factory is (good/bad) for the Derby area.
This is because ......
and ......

C

Summary   The location of industry changes over the years. These changes may affect an area in many different ways.

9 Environmental concerns

Why are we concerned about the countryside?

The countryside is a place of peace and quiet and beauty. It is a place that is different from the busy towns and cities where most people spend their lives.

For people like farmers, the countryside is a place of work. For most other people it is a place to visit and enjoy in their leisure time.

There are plenty of different things to do in the countryside. Some of these are shown in drawing **A** below.

Activities

1 Match the numbers from drawing **A** with the activities on noticeboard **B**. Answer like this:

1 = sketching

What's on today?

- sailing
- hang-gliding
- sightseeing
- walking
- picnicking
- sketching
- climbing
- canoeing
- pony-trekking
- photography
- fishing
- running

2 A hundred visitors to Keswick in the Lake District were asked what they would be doing during their stay. The results are shown in graph **C** below.
a) Give the number of people for each activity.
b) Which are the two most popular activities?

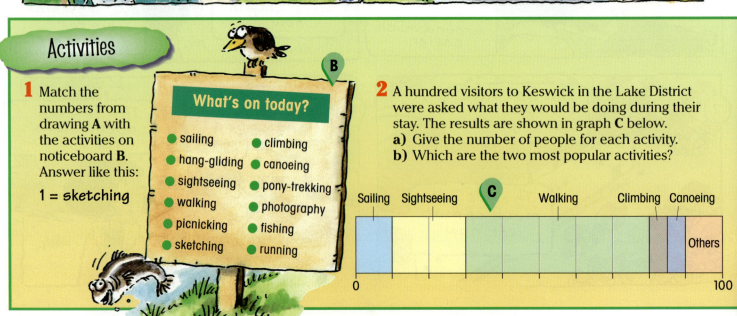

More and more people are now visiting the countryside. This has caused problems in some places.

Many of the problems are due to overcrowding. Popular sites simply attract too many people and become congested and noisy. Another problem is damage. This can affect the work of farmers and spoil the countryside for visitors.

Some of these problems are shown in drawing **D**. Look carefully and see how many you can name.

It is important to look after the countryside and treat it carefully. If we do that, others will be able to enjoy it in the future.

NOISY MOTORBOATS
CARELESS DRIVING
DAMAGED WALLS
PROBLEMS WITH DOGS
LIGHTING FIRES
GATES LEFT OPEN
DANGEROUS GAMES
FRIGHTENING ANIMALS
LITTER
DAMAGE TO FARMLAND

3 Which **two** of the activities shown in drawing **A** would you like to do? Answer like this:

- The activity I would most like to do is ....
  This is because ....
- The other activity I would like to do is ....
  This is because ....

4 a) Match each of the numbers from drawing **D** with a label from noticeboard **E**.

b) Underline the problems that would be the most damaging to plants and animals.

Summary Attractive areas of countryside are popular with visitors. This popularity may cause problems.

How can we protect the countryside?

Look at photo **A**. It shows an attractive part of the countryside in north-west England that is popular with visitors. Places like this need to be looked after and carefully **managed** if they are to remain attractive.

One of the ways that we can all help protect the countryside is to follow the **Country Code (B)**. This is a set of simple 'rules' which give advice to visitors. If followed, these rules help prevent mis-use of the countryside.

A Crummock Water in the Lake District

 B

THE COUNTRY CODE

1 Guard against all risk of fire
2 Fasten all gates
3 Keep dogs under proper control
4 Keep to the paths across farmland
5 Do not damage fences and walls

6 Leave no litter
7 Look after water supplies
8 Look after wild plants and trees
9 Go carefully on country roads
10 Respect the life of the countryside

Activities

1 Complete the postcard **C** as follows.
   a) Make a simple copy of the sketch. Put the words below in the correct places.

   - people
   - lake
   - woodland
   - grassy slopes
   - Crummock Water
   - mountains

   b) Copy and complete the sentences using the same words.

 C

Dear _____ ,

Today we are at .... The weather is good and we are having a great time. It is very pretty here. There is a ......, ... and .... to play on. We are surrounded by .... There are not many ...... here. Yesterday in Keswick it was much busier.

See you soon _____

Postcard from ....

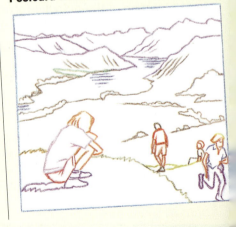

There are many people and organisations who work to protect the countryside. One of these is the **National Parks** authority.

D

The National Parks Authority

Aims
1. To protect the countryside
2. To help people enjoy the countryside

Britain's first National Parks were set up in the 1950s. They are located in some of the country's most beautiful areas. The Parks are very large and attract over 90 million visitors a year.

People who work for the National Parks are experts in **planning**, **conservation** and **land management**. They help to care for the landscape and look after the needs of visitors. They are also concerned about the people who live and work there.

E **National Parks in England and Wales**

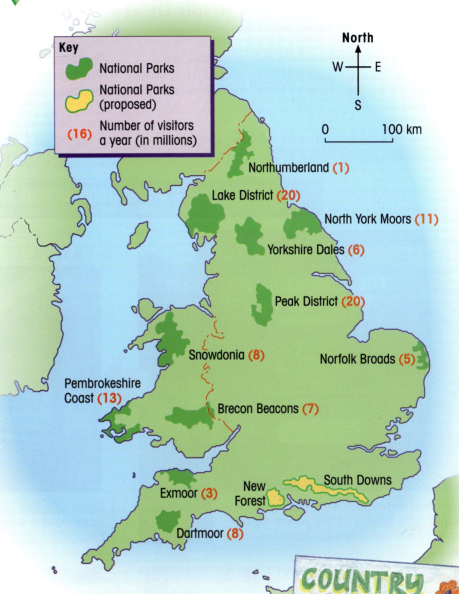

Key
- National Parks
- National Parks (proposed)
- (16) Number of visitors a year (in millions)

North
W — E
S

0   100 km

Northumberland (1)
Lake District (20)
North York Moors (11)
Yorkshire Dales (6)
Peak District (20)
Snowdonia (8)
Norfolk Broads (5)
Pembrokeshire Coast (13)
Brecon Beacons (7)
South Downs
Exmoor (3)
New Forest
Dartmoor (8)

F

2 Write sentences to answer the following.
   a) What are the two aims of National Parks?
   b) When were the Parks first set up?
   c) How many National Parks are there?
   d) How many people visit the Parks each year?
   e) Are most Parks in the north and west or the south and east?

3 a) List the National Parks in order of popularity. Put the one with the most visitors first. Give the number of visitors for each one.
   b) Underline the name of the Park nearest to where you live.

4 Make a poster to show the Country Code. Choose just three or four of the rules. Add drawings for each one.

Summary National Parks help to protect the countryside. They provide a place where people can relax and enjoy the surroundings.

What is the job of a National Park Ranger?

Rangers are employed to help look after National Parks. They are important and busy people. They work long hours and often have to work at weekends and in the evenings.

Most Rangers enjoy their work because they like the countryside.

The main job of a Ranger is to protect the Park and repair any damage to it. They also help visitors enjoy the Park, and support the needs of local people.

Sometimes they have to sort out **conflict**. Conflict is disagreement over something.

A day in the life of a National Park Ranger

1 8.30 a.m.

Start work. Sort through mail. Meeting to discuss plans for new wildlife project. Agree aim to protect rare plants and butterflies.

2 9.30 a.m.

Out to Langdale. Erect footpath signpost to direct walkers along correct right of way. Agree route with farmer. Identify any other problems.

5 1.30 p.m.

Meet with farmer. Discuss complaint about visitor-parking and damage to farmland. Agree to place new signs directing cars elsewhere.

6 2.30 p.m.

Meet with school party. Take children on guided walk. Describe surroundings. Discuss Country Code and the need to respect the countryside.

Activities

Answer all of these activities in full sentences.

1 **a)** At what time did the Ranger start work?
b) When was the last task of the day started?
c) Who was helped at 2.30 p.m.?
d) At what time was there a problem over conflict?

2 **a)** Give two examples of repair work.
b) Give two examples of help to local farmers.
c) Give two examples of help to visitors.
d) Give two examples of how the Ranger helped protect the countryside.

3 **a)** How was the bridge damaged?
b) What was the likely cause of footpath erosion?
c) What damage was the farmer worried about?
d) Why is it good for children to learn the Country Code?

Summary

National Park Rangers help look after the countryside. They are also concerned with the needs of visitors and local people.

3 **11.00 a.m.**

Meet National Trust Warden. Discuss how visitors might be helped to enjoy and support the Park.

4 **12.00 midday**

The National Trust
EROSION CONTROL IN PROGRESS
Please keep to footpath

Inspect badly eroded (worn away) path. Discuss with volunteer workers how it may be repaired. Agree costs and when to start.

7 **4.00 p.m.**

Back to Langdale. Join bridge-building team. Help repair damage caused by recent flood. Order extra timber.

8 **7.30 p.m.**

Tourist Information

Keswick in the evening. Give slide show and talk on the Lake District National Park. Over 100 visitors and many local people in audience.

How can we measure the quality of the environment?

The **environment** is everything around us.
● It includes **human features** like houses, factories, roads and towns.
● It also includes **natural features** like hills, valleys, lakes, weather and wildlife.
● These natural features are called the **physical environment**.
● Another word for environment is **surroundings**.

The countryside is part of the environment. It is a place where people, plants and animals live. As we have seen, it can easily be spoilt and damaged if it is not looked after carefully.

An **environmental survey** can be used to measure the quality of a place. It can also help identify problems and damage. It can then be used to help solve the problems and improve the surroundings.

Activities

1 a) Make a copy of the survey sheet below.
 b) Complete a survey for photo **A**.
 c) Tick the points you would give for each feature.
 d) Add up the total number of points.

2 Repeat activity **1** for photos **B** and **C**.

3 Look at your points totals. The higher the number, the better the quality.
 a) Which place has the highest quality of environment?
 b) Which place has the lowest quality of environment?

4 a) List three good features about the best place.
 b) List three bad features about the worst place.

5 Imagine that you are a National Park Ranger. What three things would you do to help improve the place with the poorest quality of environment?

6 a) Complete an environmental survey for an area around your school or home.
 b) Suggest how the area may be improved.

Points are given for each feature.
For example:

● If a place is very attractive it will score 5 points.
● If it is ugly it will score 1 point.
● If it is in between it will score 2, 3 or 4 points.

QUALITY OF ENVIRONMENT SURVEY SHEET

	High quality				Low quality	
	5	4	3	2	1	
Attractive						Ugly
Peaceful						Busy
Clean						Dirty
Tidy						Untidy
Special						Ordinary
Safe						Dangerous
No cars						Many cars
Well kept						Poorly kept
Interesting						Boring
Like						Dislike

Place .... Total ...... out of 50

A Derwent Water, Keswick

B

Little Town, near Keswick

C Blencathra, near Keswick

Summary

The quality of the environment may be measured using a survey. This can help identify good points and bad points.

How can we use a writing frame?

As we have seen on pages 90 and 91, we can measure the quality of the landscape by completing an **environmental survey**. This involves giving a number of different features a score. When added together, these scores give a measure of the quality of environment.

A geography class were interested in the area around their school. They visited the places in the photos below and completed an environmental survey sheet for each one. They then wrote a report on their findings.

They wrote the report using a **writing frame**. A writing frame provides a framework on which to base our writing. It helps us plan our sentences and paragraphs. It also makes sure that we keep closely to the topic or issue that we are studying.

Drawing **E** is a writing frame. We can use it to describe the good points and bad points about an area. It can then help us to suggest how the environment may be improved.

A West Road shops and congestion

B College entrance

C Terraced housing

D Open land

Writing frame

Report on quality of the environment

My class conducted an environmental survey of the area around the school. The survey shows that the quality of environment varies from one place to another.

The two places with the highest quality of environment are ....

The two places with the lowest quality are ....

The three best features of the area are ....

The three worst features of the area are ....

The environmental survey has shown that the area has a number of environmental problems. These include
....

I think these environmental problems could be reduced by
....

Activities

1 Write a quality of environment report for the area shown in the photos **A**, **B**, **C** and **D**.
- Use the writing frame for your report.
- The survey results for each place are show in drawing **F**.
- Some suggestions for improving the area are given below.

- Pedestrianise the busiest areas
- Replace old houses with modern new ones
- Introduce a clean-up scheme
- Make waste ground into play areas

2 Complete a quality of environmental survey for your school grounds. Survey at least four different places. Use writing frame **E** to report on your findings.

QUALITY OF ENVIRONMENT SURVEY SHEET

Place	A	B	C	D	
Attractive	5	2	2	4	Ugly
Peaceful	4	1	2	5	Busy
Clean	5	2	2	4	Dirty
Tidy	5	1	2	3	Untidy
Special	4	2	1	3	Ordinary
Safe	5	1	3	4	Dangerous
No cars	5	1	3	2	Many cars
Well kept	5	2	1	3	Poorly kept
Interesting	4	3	1	3	Boring
Like	4	3	1	3	Dislike
Total	**46**	**18**	**18**	**34**	**out of 50**

Features are scored from 1 to 5.
The higher the score, the better the environment.

Summary

A writing frame provides a framework for a piece of work. It helps us to plan and structure our writing.

Where on Earth do we live?

People are not spread evenly over the world. Some places are crowded and some have very few people.

Map **A** below shows this spread of people. It is a **population distribution** map. Look carefully at Europe and South-east Asia. Notice how crowded they are. Australasia and most of Africa are different. They have very few people.

The reason for this uneven distribution is that some places are more suitable to live in than others.

The most crowded places of all are towns and cities. These places are becoming more and more popular places to live. This is because they provide the things that most people need in their lives.

HOUSE FOR SALE

Hot, cold, dry, wet, flat, hilly ... Oh dear, where on Earth shall I go?

A   Where people live in the world

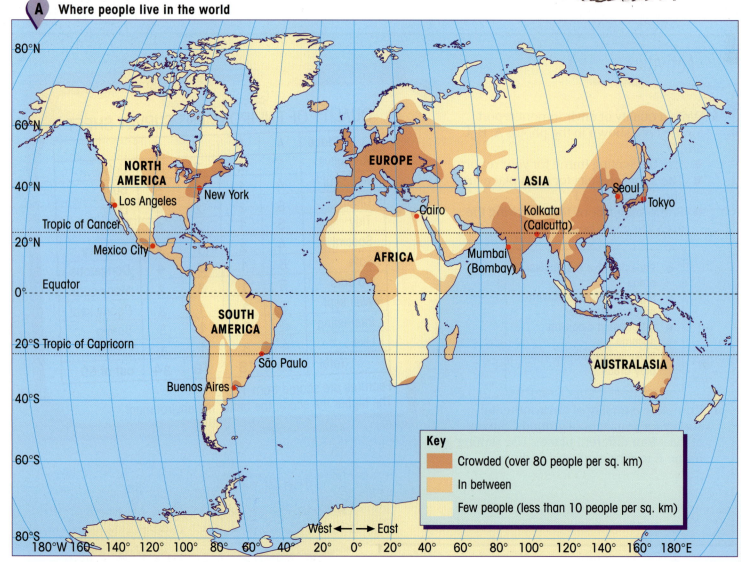

Key

Crowded (over 80 people per sq. km)

In between

Few people (less than 10 people per sq. km)

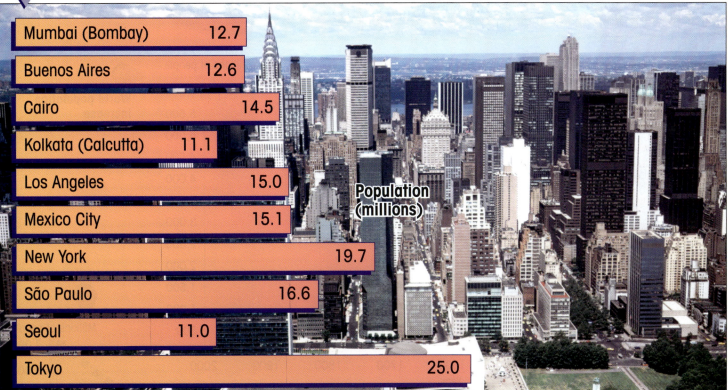

City	Population (millions)
Mumbai (Bombay)	12.7
Buenos Aires	12.6
Cairo	14.5
Kolkata (Calcutta)	11.1
Los Angeles	15.0
Mexico City	15.1
New York	19.7
São Paulo	16.6
Seoul	11.0
Tokyo	25.0

Activities

1 Look at map **A**. Of the six statements below, four are correct. Write out the correct ones.
- People are not spread evenly over the world.
- People are spread evenly over Asia.
- Some places in the world are more crowded than others.
- Europe is a crowded continent.
- South America is the most crowded continent.
- Africa is a continent with few people.

2 Make a copy of table **C**.
- **a)** In column 1 list the cities in order of size (graph **B**). Give the largest first.
- **b)** In column 2 give the population for each city.
- **c)** In column 3 name the continent they are in (map **A**). The first one has been done for you.

3 Look at map **A**. Name the cities at each of the following locations. The first one has been done for you.
- **a)** 38°N 127°E = *Seoul*
- **b)** 36°N 140°E =
- **c)** 23°N 88°E =
- **d)** 19°N 73°E =
- **e)** 24°S 47°W =
- **f)** 34°S 58°W =

4 Give the **latitude** and **longitude** for the cities below. Answer like this:
- **a)** Mexico City = *19°N 99°W*
- **b)** New York =
- **c)** Los Angeles =
- **d)** Cairo =

C

① City	② Population	③ Continent
1 Tokyo	25.0 million	Asia
2		
3		
4		

Summary

People are spread unevenly over the world. More and more people are living in cities.

How does population change?

The number of people in the world has been increasing very quickly. Only two hundred years ago there were 1,000 million people. Now there are over 6,000 million. By 2045 there may be 10,000 million.

Look carefully at graph **A**. Notice how slow the growth was at first. Only recently has there been a rapid increase or 'explosion'.

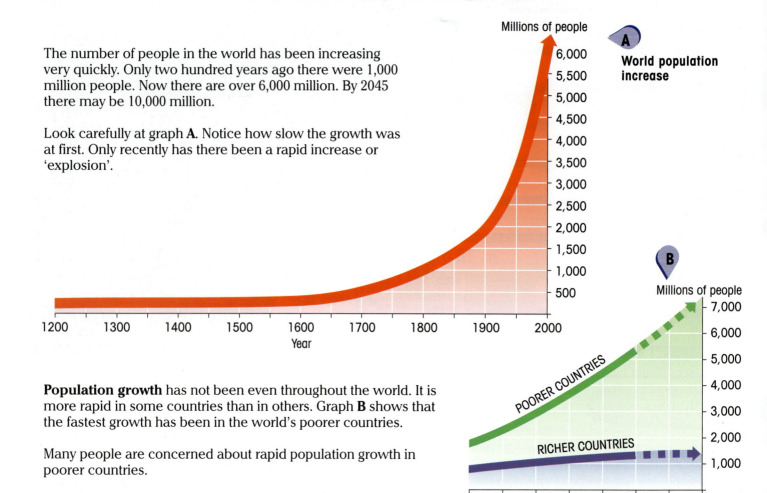

A World population increase

Population growth has not been even throughout the world. It is more rapid in some countries than in others. Graph **B** shows that the fastest growth has been in the world's poorer countries.

Many people are concerned about rapid population growth in poorer countries.

They worry about overcrowding, food shortages and disease. Increased poverty and a poor **quality of life** are also problems.

Activities

1 Look at graph **A**. Give the population for each of these years. Answer like this:
Year 1200 = 250 million   Year 1800 = ...
Year 1400 = ...   Year 2000 = ...
Year 1600 = ...

2 Look carefully at graph **A**. Match the following beginnings to the correct endings.

Up to about 1600	– very rapid growth
1600 to 1800	– growing very slowly
From about 1800	– beginning to grow quickly

3 Look at graph **B**.
Write out the following statements.
Next to each one say if it is **True** or **False**.

- Nearly 5,000 million people now live in poor countries.
- 7,000 million people now live in rich countries.
- About 1,000 million people now live in rich countries.
- All countries have the same growth rate.
- The poorer countries are growing rapidly.
- The richer countries are growing slowly.
- World population growth is uneven.
- Population growth affects quality of life.

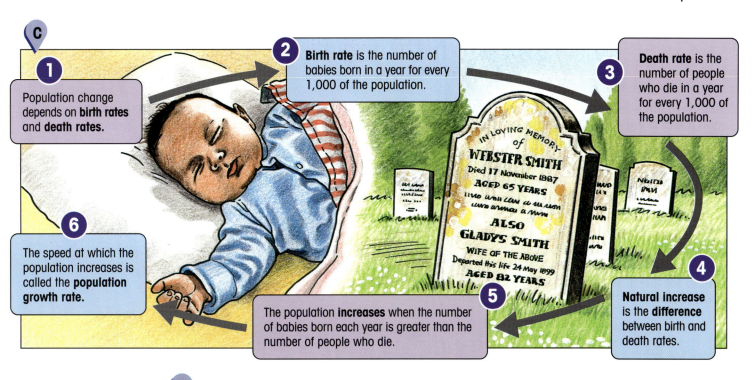

C

1 Population change depends on **birth rates** and **death rates**.

2 **Birth rate** is the number of babies born in a year for every 1,000 of the population.

3 **Death rate** is the number of people who die in a year for every 1,000 of the population.

6 The speed at which the population increases is called the **population growth rate**.

5 The population **increases** when the number of babies born each year is greater than the number of people who die.

4 **Natural increase** is the **difference** between birth and death rates.

D

Birth rate greater than death rate → Population growth

Birth rate same as death rate → Population steady

Birth rate less than death rate → Population decline

E

Country	Birth rate	Death rate	Natural increase
China	21	7	14
India	31	10	21
Italy	11	10	1
Japan	12	8	4
Kenya	47	10	37
Mexico	17	6	11
UK	14	12	2
USA	14	9	5

---

4 Look at table **E**. Which country has:
   a) The highest birth rate?
   b) The highest death rate?
   c) The smallest natural increase?
   d) The largest natural increase?
   e) The slowest population growth?
   f) The most rapid population growth?

5 Look at photo **F**.
   a) What problem does it show?
   b) Give two other problems that may result from rapid population growth.

F

Queueing for food in Sudan, a poor country with rapid population growth

Summary

The population of the world is increasing very quickly. Growth is fastest in the poorer countries.

What is migration?

We have already seen that **birth rates** and **death rates** can affect population. Another way that the population may change is by **migration**.

> Migration is the movement of people from one place to another to live and work.

There are two main reasons why people migrate. Some people move because life is difficult where they live. Others want to go to a place which they hope will be better for them. These reasons are called **push and pull factors**.

Many people in the world move from the countryside to cities. This is called **rural-to-urban** migration. Movement like this causes cities to grow very quickly. It is most common in the poorer countries of the world.

Mexico is one of the world's poorer countries. Its capital, Mexico City, attracts many **migrants** and is one of the fastest-growing cities in the world.

Estimates suggest that very soon there will be over 30 million people living in Mexico City. This will make it the biggest city in the world.

Push factors make people want to leave an area.

Pull factors attract people to an area

A Push and pull factors

PULL FACTORS

Hope for:
- Chance of a job
- Better housing
- Education
- Medical care
- Improved conditions
- Better way of life
- Family links

- Not enough jobs
- Few opportunities
- Lack of food
- Shortage of land
- Political fears
- Difficult conditions

TO A BETTER WAY OF LIFE

PUSH FACTORS

Activities

1 Make a copy of table **B**.
Tick each factor to show if it is **push** or **pull**.

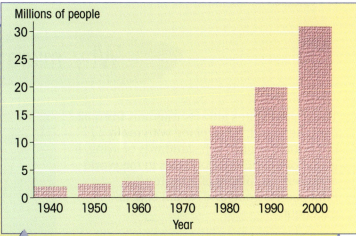

D **Mexico City – population growth**

B

Factor	Push	Pull
No hospitals		
Work available		
Plenty to do		
No schools		
No work		
Better quality of life		
Some good housing		
Unhappy life		

2 Look at figure **C**. Say why each of the migrants moved, by answering **push**, **pull** or **push and pull**.
Answer like this: **1 = push and pull**

3 Look at graph **D**.
  a) What was the population in 1940?
  b) When did the population reach 10 million?
  c) What is the population for 2000?
  d) Is the population growth slow, steady or rapid?
  e) Why is Mexico City growing so much?

Summary   Migration is the movement of people from one place to live in another. It is affected by push and pull factors.

C **Reasons for migration to Mexico City**

99

Why migrate to America?

The United States attracts migrants from all over the world. It is a place with many opportunities and high standards of living. It is one of the richest countries in the world and there are plenty of jobs there. Education is good and health care is excellent.

Just across the border to the south lies a different world. Mexico is a poor country and life can be very difficult there. Poverty, a lack of jobs and poor living conditions are the biggest problems.

Many Mexicans have migrated to the USA. They go in search of jobs and a chance to make money. Their main aim is to improve the quality of their lives.

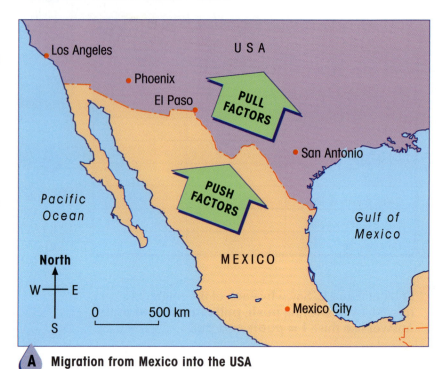

A Migration from Mexico into the USA

B The USA and Mexico compared

Jobs

% of people in full-time work

Mexico 55% USA 93%

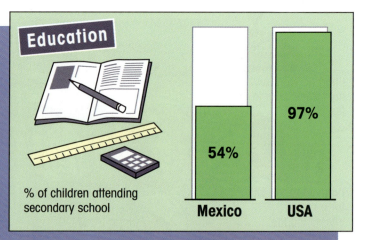

Education

% of children attending secondary school

Mexico 54% USA 97%

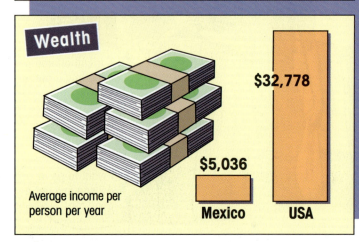

Wealth

Average income per person per year

$32,778 USA
$5,036 Mexico

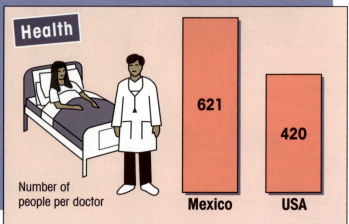

Health

Number of people per doctor

Mexico 621 USA 420

C **Storyboard: A Mexican family discuss their future**

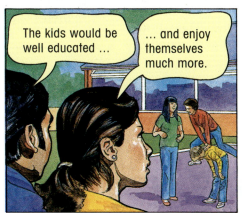

Activities

1 Match the following beginnings with the correct endings.

a) A Mexican family living in Mexico

We are not happy	is poor in Mexico
Only half our people	a good education
We earn	have a proper job
Our children do not have	with our life in Mexico
Health care	very poor wages

b) A Mexican family thinking of living in America

9 out of 10 people	would be better in America
We would earn	get a good education
There are lots of doctors	have a job in America
Our children would	so health care is good
Our quality of life	much higher wages

2 These Mexicans want to go to America. Copy and complete the sentences to explain why they want to go. Include at least two facts from graphs **B** for each.

A family man with elderly parents

I want to go to America because ......
and ......

A brother and sister aged 12 and 16

We want to go to America because ......
and ......

Summary

The United States has much to offer migrants. Many Mexicans move there in the hope of gaining employment and finding a better chance in life.

What are the effects of migration?

Over 12 million Mexican migrants now live in the United States. This has brought some benefits but has also caused problems. Strict controls have now been introduced to prevent illegal entry and to reduce the problems.

Despite these controls, more than 300,000 people still manage to cross the border from Mexico every year. Many Mexicans are happy with their new life in America. Others have found life more difficult.

Look at the comments with photo **A** below. They show how some Mexicans have got on in their new country.

Activities

1 Look at the statements with photo **A** below. For each one say if you think it is good or bad for a **migrant**. Answer like this: **1** = *good*

2 Imagine that you are a Mexican and have migrated to America. Do you think you would like it there? Give three reasons for your answer.

A Some views of Mexican migrants living in America

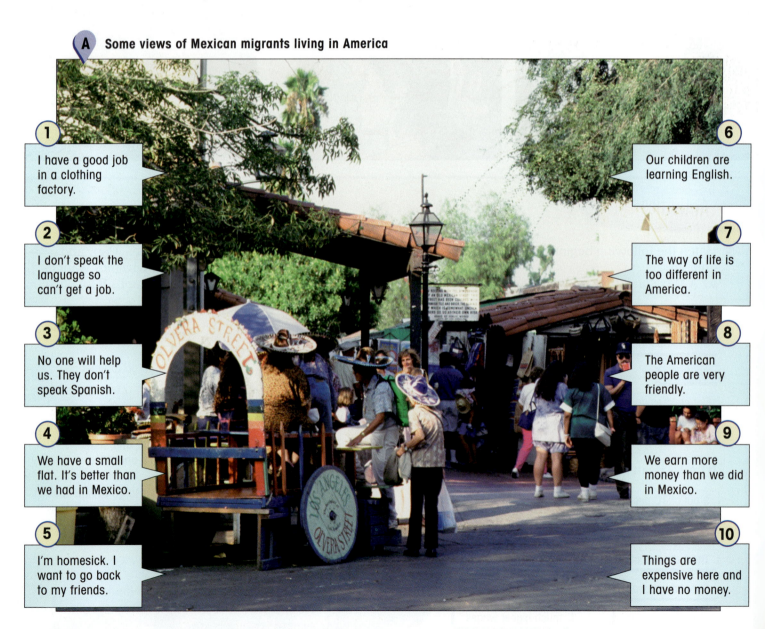

1 I have a good job in a clothing factory.

2 I don't speak the language so can't get a job.

3 No one will help us. They don't speak Spanish.

4 We have a small flat. It's better than we had in Mexico.

5 I'm homesick. I want to go back to my friends.

6 Our children are learning English.

7 The way of life is too different in America.

8 The American people are very friendly.

9 We earn more money than we did in Mexico.

10 Things are expensive here and I have no money.

Large-scale migrations can affect countries in many ways. Mexico, for example, is concerned that some of its best workers are leaving the country. This causes problems for new industries trying to set up in the country.

For America the situation is different. The migrants have increased the population and introduced a Mexican way of life to the cities. They have helped America get rich but have caused a few problems as well.

Look at the comments with photo **B** below. They show some of the ways that migration can affect a country.

Activities

3 Look at the statements with photo **B** below. For each one say if you think it is good or bad for the American people.
Answer like this: **11** = *bad*

4 Imagine that you are an American living just across the border from Mexico. Would you be for or against Mexican migrants? Give three reasons for your answer.

Summary

There are many effects of migration. Some are good and some are bad. Some affect the migrants and others affect the place they move to.

B   **Some American views on Mexican migrants**

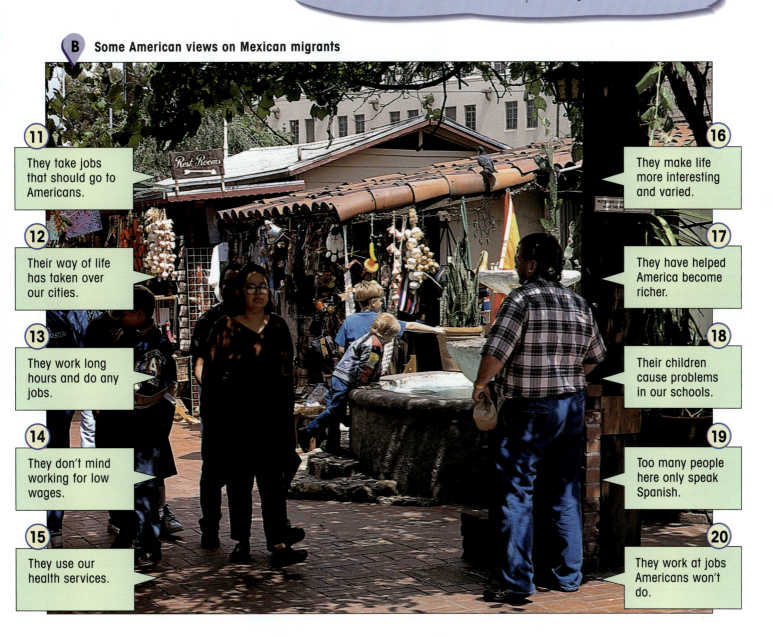

11 They take jobs that should go to Americans.

12 Their way of life has taken over our cities.

13 They work long hours and do any jobs.

14 They don't mind working for low wages.

15 They use our health services.

16 They make life more interesting and varied.

17 They have helped America become richer.

18 Their children cause problems in our schools.

19 Too many people here only speak Spanish.

20 They work at jobs Americans won't do.

11 Kenya

What are Kenya's main features?

Kenya is in East Africa on the **Equator**. It is an attractive country with a wide variety of scenery and wildlife. Inland there are snow-covered mountains, lakes, grassy plains and a wealth of wildlife. On the coast there are sandy beaches and coral reefs.

These features attract large numbers of tourists to Kenya. Many go on organised tours called **safaris** where they view animals in their natural surroundings. Kenya has over 50 **National Parks** and **game reserves** where animals are protected and tourism is encouraged.

After a safari, most people go to the coast to relax. Here they can stay in comfortable beach resorts and enjoy hot and sunny weather throughout the year.

A The giraffe orphanage in Nairobi

B Kenya – main features

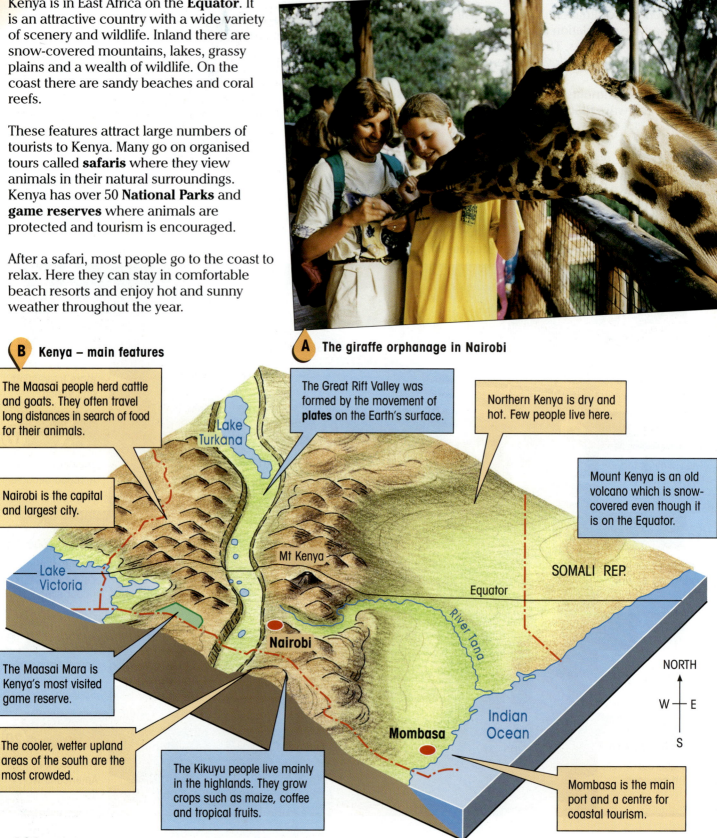

The Maasai people herd cattle and goats. They often travel long distances in search of food for their animals.

The Great Rift Valley was formed by the movement of **plates** on the Earth's surface.

Northern Kenya is dry and hot. Few people live here.

Mount Kenya is an old volcano which is snow-covered even though it is on the Equator.

Nairobi is the capital and largest city.

The Maasai Mara is Kenya's most visited game reserve.

The cooler, wetter upland areas of the south are the most crowded.

The Kikuyu people live mainly in the highlands. They grow crops such as maize, coffee and tropical fruits.

Mombasa is the main port and a centre for coastal tourism.

Lake Turkana

Lake Victoria

Mt Kenya

SOMALI REP.

Equator

River Tana

Nairobi

Mombasa

Indian Ocean

NORTH
W — E
S

Kenya is more than twice the size of Britain but has less than half the number of people. Large parts of the country are almost empty. The most crowded places are around the towns and in the few areas that can be farmed easily.

Many different people make up Kenya's population. Amongst the most well-known tribes are the Maasai and the Kikuyu. These people live very simple lives and nearly all of them are farmers.

However, farming is difficult. There is a shortage of good, fertile land, and 80 per cent of the country is too dry to grow crops. Poor transport and bad roads make it difficult for farmers to get their products to the market.

Producing enough food for a rapidly increasing population is Kenya's biggest problem.

C A Kikuyu dancer

D Maasai people

Activities

1 Look at drawing **B** and map **E**. Match the following features with a number from map **E**. The first one has been done for you.

- **Nairobi 1**
- Mombasa ...
- Mount Kenya ...
- Lake Victoria ...
- Lake Turkana ...
- Great Rift Valley ...
- River Tana ...
- Equator ...

E

```
SUDAN          ETHIOPIA

                    3

UGANDA                      SOMALI
                            REP.
            7

        4           2
6
        1
                    5
                            North
                          W —+— E
TANZANIA            8        S

    0      200 km
```

2 Look at drawing **B** and photos **C** and **D**. Make a copy of table **F** and sort the following into the correct columns. Some may be used more than once.

- Brightly coloured clothes
- Wear many beads
- Grow crops
- Live in highlands
- Very dark skins
- Herd cattle and goats
- Live in cooler, wetter areas
- Travel long distances

F

Kikuyu people	Maasai people
●	●

3 Copy and complete this paragraph.
Kenya is on Africa's ...... coast. It has two main towns. The capital is ...... and ...... is a port on the ...... Ocean. The highest mountain is Mount .... Two of Kenya's tribes are the ...... and .... The main occupation of these people is ....

Summary

Kenya has a wealth of beautiful scenery and interesting wildlife. Its people belong to many different tribal groups, and farming is their main occupation.

105

How developed is Kenya?

All countries are different. For example, some are rich and have high **standards of living**. Others are poor and have lower standards of living. Countries that differ in this way are said to be at different stages of **development**.

The UK is an example of a rich country and is said to be **developed**. Kenya, on the other hand, is a poor country. It is still **developing**.

Development can be measured in many different ways. The most common and easiest method is by measuring wealth. This can be misleading, though. In the UK, for example, there are many people who live in bad housing or are homeless – just as in Kenya. In fact all countries, whether they are wealthy or not, have some poor people living in them.

A more important measure of development is **quality of life**. Many Kenyans, despite living in poor conditions, are cheerful, relaxed and always willing to help others. Socially they appear more developed and happier than many people in the so-called 'richer' countries.

Our country is making progress but most of us are still very poor.

We still need better roads, a clean, reliable water supply and more food.

For most of us life in Kenya is very difficult.

A

Activities

1 Use figure **C** for this activity. Write either **Kenya** or **the UK** to complete these sentences.

- In ...... most people have plenty to eat.
- In ...... few people have cars.
- In ...... people have difficulty getting a doctor.
- In ...... most children go to school.

2 Figure **C** will help you with this activity.
  a) Of the six sentences below, three are correct. Write them out.
  b) Correct the other three sentences then write them out.

- Kenya is richer than the UK.
- People in the UK have more food than they need.
- Kenya is a developed country.
- The UK is a developing country.
- Health care in the UK is better than in Kenya.
- Few people are able to watch TV in Kenya.

3 Kenya is one of the poorer countries in the world. In some ways, though, it may be seen as a rich country. Which of these statements suggest that Kenya is rich, and which suggest that it is poor?
Answer like this **1** = *poor*

B

1 Low wages	6 Happy people
2 Cheerful outlook	7 Poor health care
3 Friendly to visitors	8 Not enough schools
4 Food shortages	9 Beautiful countryside
5 Few cars	10 Helpful attitudes

Summary

Kenya is a developing country and its people are very poor. Despite this, many enjoy a good quality of life.

C Development: Kenya and the UK compared

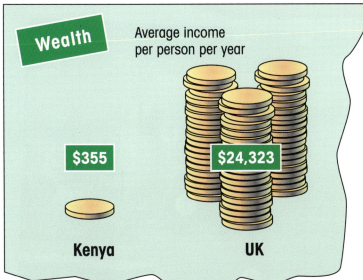

Wealth — Average income per person per year

$355 Kenya
$24,323 UK

Food — Daily calorie supply as % of needs

89% Kenya
130% UK

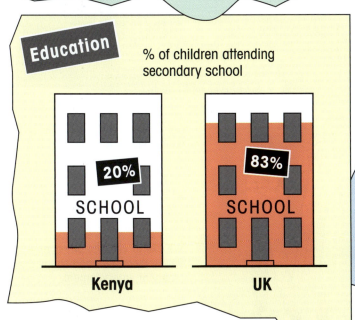

Education — % of children attending secondary school

20% SCHOOL Kenya
83% SCHOOL UK

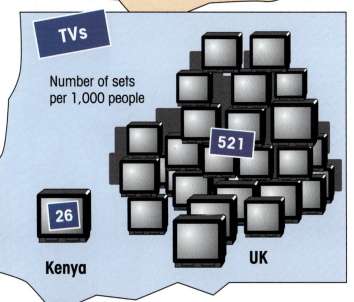

TVs — Number of sets per 1,000 people

26 Kenya
521 UK

Health — Number of people per doctor

10,130 Kenya
300 UK

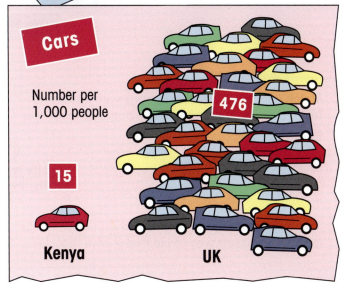

Cars — Number per 1,000 people

15 Kenya
476 UK

Nairobi: the rich ...

Nairobi is Kenya's capital and one of the largest cities in East Africa. In its centre are many government buildings, tall office blocks and luxury hotels. Several international organisations are also based there.

Uhuru Park is a large area of open space near the city centre. Nearby are some of Nairobi's most expensive houses.

A

Nairobi – the city centre

Our parents both work in the city centre and have well-paid jobs.

We live in a lovely home with air-conditioning and a large garden.

There are four of us in the family so there is plenty of space for us all.

We have two cars, a TV and many modern gadgets.

B

Our house has a high fence and a good security system.

We attend private schools but will soon go to Nairobi University.

We like to visit the city centre where there are good shops and plenty of entertainment.

The Mujava family

Activities

1 Match each of these descriptions with a number from photo **A**. The first one has been done for you.
- Main road = 1
- City centre =
- Tall office block =
- Parkland =
- Lake =

C

Life in a shanty town

2 The Mujava family are very wealthy. List five things about their way of life that shows this.

3 The Ongeera family are very poor. Answer these questions using full sentences.

A Where does the family live?

B Why are people there so poor?

C What is the house made from?

D Why is the house so crowded?

E Why is scrap material so useful?

F How many rooms does the house have?

... and the poor

Nairobi now has a population of over two million and is growing rapidly.

Most of this growth is due to **migrants** leaving the countryside and looking for a better life in the city.

This has caused many problems. When the migrants arrive they have no jobs, no money and nowhere to live.

Most settle in areas of slum housing on the edge of the city. These are called **shanty towns**.

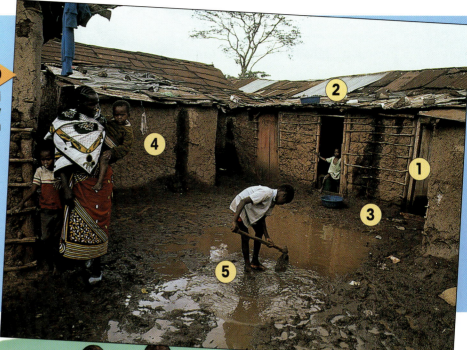

D A Nairobi shanty town

We live in a shanty town on the edge of Nairobi.

No one here has a proper job so we are all very poor.

Our home is made of mud and corrugated iron.

We have no running water but hope to get electricity soon.

Seven of us live here all in one room. It's a bit crowded but we manage.

There is an open sewer outside our door and rubbish lies everywhere.

We are quite skilful and are always making things from scrap to use in the home or sell at the market.

E

The Ongeera family

4 Match each of these descriptions with a number from photo **D**. The first one has been done for you.
- **Houses close together** = 1
- Mud walls =
- Corrugated iron roofs =
- Open sewers =
- Dirty conditions =

5 Copy and complete the paragraph below using the words from drawing **F**.
An area of slum housing is called a .... It is an area of poor-quality housing which often lacks ...... and .... Shanty towns are the result of ...... coming to the ....

F

Summary

In Nairobi the rich are very rich and the poor are very poor. This makes life good for the few who are rich. For the majority who are poor, however, life can be very difficult.

How is tea grown in the Kericho region?

To the west of the Rift Valley lies the town of Kericho. The area was once covered in forests but these have now been cleared to grow tea.

Brooke Bond have a huge tea **plantation** near Kericho. The estate stretches many miles across rolling hills. The bright-green tea bushes are planted in long straight rows. The leaves are picked by hand. This means that many people are needed to collect the crop.

Brooke Bond employs 16,000 workers. Most of them live with their families on the estate.

The tea produced is **exported** all over the world. This has brought money into Kenya and has helped to improve living standards.

A Tea plantation in Kericho

Activities

1 Mapskills 2 on page 57 will help you with this activity. Measure these distances on map **C** using the scale-line.
  a) Kericho to Kisumu
  b) Kericho to Nairobi
  c) Kericho to Mombasa
  d) Nairobi to Mombasa

2 Complete the quizword using the clues given.

3 List five things about the Kericho district that make it good for tea growing.

4 Give five reasons why a Kenyan may like to work on the Brooke Bond tea estate at Kericho.

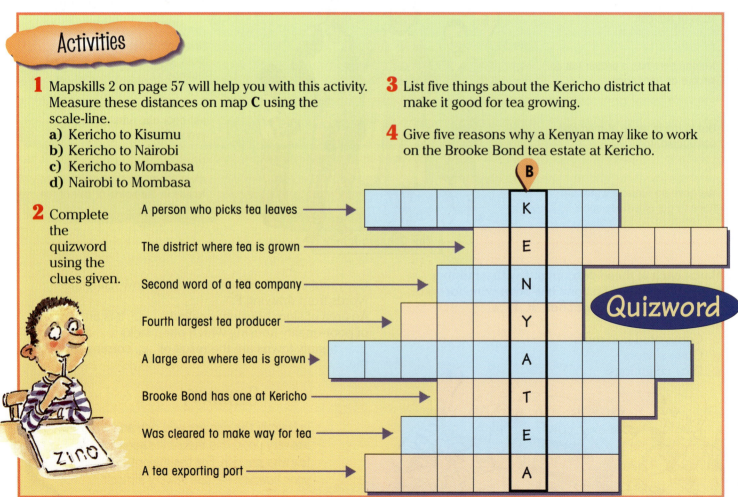

A person who picks tea leaves ⟶ K

The district where tea is grown ⟶ E

Second word of a tea company ⟶ N

Fourth largest tea producer ⟶ Y

A large area where tea is grown ⟶ A

Brooke Bond has one at Kericho ⟶ T

Was cleared to make way for tea ⟶ E

A tea exporting port ⟶ A

Quizword

C The Kericho district

- A hilly area about 2,000 m above sea level.
- A cool, damp climate with plenty of sunshine.
- Gentle slopes and good volcanic soil.
- Ideal conditions for growing tea bushes.
- Tea transported by road and rail from Kericho.
- Tea exported by ship from Kisumu and Mombasa.

D The pluckers

- The people who pick the leaves are called pluckers.
- The leaves are carefully picked by hand.
- They are put into large baskets on the plucker's back.
- The plucker is paid by the weight of leaves picked.
- Pluckers return to the same bush every 18 days.
- The bushes are kept one metre high.

E The tea estate

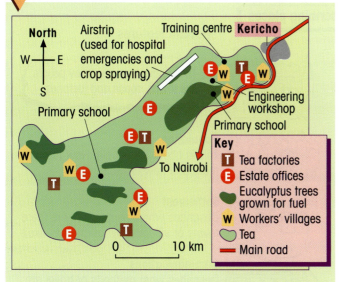

- Work starts at 7 o'clock in the morning.
- Pluckers work a nine-hour day with two short breaks.
- Earnings are about 45p per day.
- Free housing, education and medical care are provided.
- The houses have water, electricity and sewerage.
- The estate has shops and other amenities.
- Over 100,000 people live on the estate.

F The tea industry

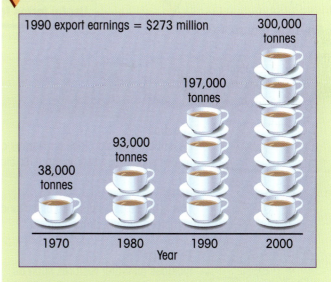

- Very high-quality tea is produced.
- Demand for Kenya tea has increased rapidly.
- Most tea is grown on large **commercial** plantations.
- Small farmers also produce large amounts of tea.
- The Government plans to further increase production.
- Kenya is now the world's fourth largest tea producer.

Summary The highland areas of Kenya are ideal for tea production. Tea is now Kenya's most valuable export.

How can we describe places?

Look at photos C and D on the next page. They show two different places in Kenya. Knowing how to describe places like these is an important skill in geography.

A good way to describe a place is to follow the three easy steps shown in drawing A below.
Drawing B shows some geographical terms that we can use to describe places. Not all of the terms need to be used all of the time. Sometimes you may only use the ones important to your study.

1 Look carefully at the information you have.
2 List the geographical terms that can be used to describe the area.
3 Write a sentence or two about each of the terms.

A

Look

1 Look carefully at the information you have.

List

2 List the geographical terms that can be used to describe the area.

Write

3 Write a sentence or two about each of the terms.

B

Useful terms for describing places

Physical features

These are natural features such as mountains, rivers and lakes.

Location
Describes where a place is. Names of places should be used where possible.

Relief
This is the height and shape of the land. Is it steep, gently sloping or flat?

Drainage
Includes all water features such as streams, rivers, lakes and marshes.

Climate
Describes the weather conditions such as temperature, rainfall and sunshine.

Vegetation
Describes the plant life and includes forest, grassland and farmed areas.

Human features

These have been made by people, like towns, roads and factories.

Population
This is about the people. How many are there and how crowded is it?

Settlement
Describes where people live. Are there towns or villages? What are they like?

Communications
Describes what methods of travel are available. Is travel easy or difficult?

Work or employment
This is what people do for a living. What sorts of jobs are people likely to do?

Conclusion
This gives a summary and may say what we think about the place.

C Luo village, Lake Victoria

D Mara River, Maasai Mara

Activities

1 Look at photo C. Complete these sentences to describe Luo village. Include the words given below.
  a) The location is …
  b) The relief is a …
  c) The drainage feature is …
  d) The climate seems to be …
  e) The vegetation has mostly been …
  f) The people live in a …
  g) Communications will be mainly by …
  h) The people make a living from …

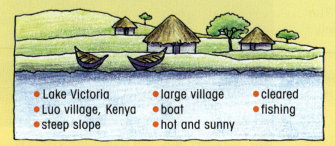

- Lake Victoria
- Luo village, Kenya
- steep slope
- large village
- boat
- hot and sunny
- cleared
- fishing

2 Look at photo D.
  a) List the geographical terms below.
  b) Add two or three more terms to your list.
  c) Write a sentence about each of the terms.

- Location: ………………………
- Relief: ………………………
- Drainage: ………………………
- Climate: ………………………
- ………………………………
- ………………………………

3 Describe Nairobi using information from pages 108 and 109.

Summary

A place can be described by setting out a list of geographical terms then writing about each one in turn.

What are tropical rainforests?

A The River Xingu winding through the Amazon rainforest in Brazil

Look at photo **A** above – a huge area of thick forest stretching as far as the eye can see.

Forests like this are called **tropical rainforests**. They cover large areas of the Earth's surface and grow in places that are very hot and wet.

There are several rainforests around the world. They all lie close to the Equator where there are high temperatures and plenty of rain all year round.

These conditions help the plants to grow easily and quickly. The thick and varied **vegetation** provides a home for a huge variety of **wildlife**.

There are more than 5 million different types of plants, animals, birds and insects in the forest. Some of the trees are more than 40 metres high and weigh over 100 tonnes.

Much of the wildlife has yet to be identified and recorded. This is because the forest is so dense and so large that many places have still not been visited.

B The larger trees have huge buttress roots to support them. This is because the underground part of the root is very shallow.

114

C

The tallest trees grow high above the tree-tops. They have small leaves to reduce the loss of moisture in the wind. The larger birds and many animals live here.

D

Most trees have climbers growing round them. Rope-like lianas grow upwards from the forest floor. Other plants collect moisture by dangling their roots in the humid air.

E

The forest is full of unusual animals, birds and insects. They make a lot of noise. Some are deadly. The rainforest can be a frightening and dangerous place for those who don't know it.

Activities

1 Match the following beginnings with the correct endings.

Buttress roots	grow round tree branches
Large trees	is a dangerous place
The rainforest	support large trees
Large birds	often have shallow roots
Lianas	live at the tops of trees

2 Copy and complete these sentences.
   a) Plants grow quickly and easily in the rainforest because ......
   b) There is plenty of wildlife in the rainforest because ......
   c) Some of the wildlife is still not known because ......

3 Write a short paragraph to describe photo **A**. Include the words below. Start like this:
The Amazon rainforest is ......

| mainly flat | a few hills | winding river |
| thick forest | no open space | |

Summary   Tropical rainforests are hot and wet. They have more plants and wildlife than anywhere else on Earth.

Where are the tropical rainforests?

Tropical rainforests need a climate that is hot and wet all year. There should also be many hours of sunshine and daylight. Conditions like this may be found in places with an **equatorial climate**.

In the rainforest the weather is the same almost every day of the year:
● Fine in the morning.
● Very heavy rainstorms, often with thunder and lightning, in the afternoon.
● Warm and still in the evening.

Look at climate graph **B** for Manaus. It is in the Amazon rainforest and has an equatorial climate.

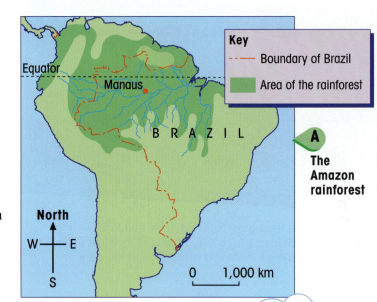

A The Amazon rainforest

B Climate graph for Manaus

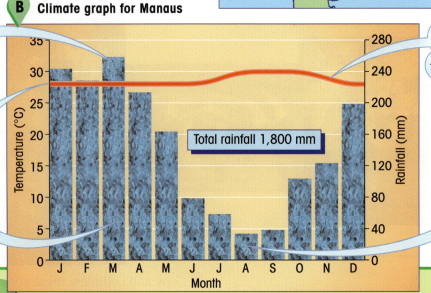

Notice that some months are very wet indeed.

Notice how warm it is all year.

Notice that there is plenty of rain in every month of the year.

Notice how the temperature is about the same all year round.

Notice that even in the drier months there is still quite a lot of rain.

Total rainfall 1,800 mm

Activities

1 Look at the rainfall bars on climate graph **B** above.
  a) Which is the wettest month?
  b) Which is the driest month?
  c) Which months have more than 200 mm of rain?
  d) Which months have less than 100 mm of rain?

2 Look at the temperature line on graph **B**.
  a) What is the highest temperature?
  b) What is the lowest temperature?
  c) What is the difference between the highest and lowest temperatures?

3 Look at the drawings and descriptions in **C** below. They show a typical rainforest day but are in the wrong order. Write out the descriptions in the correct order.

C

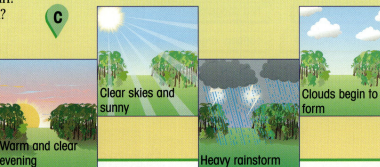

Clear skies and sunny

Clouds begin to form

Warm and clear evening

Heavy rainstorm

As you can see from map **D**, tropical rainforests are found close to the Equator in South-east Asia, Africa and South America.

The Amazon is the largest rainforest. It stretches almost 4,000 km from east to west and 2,000 km from north to south. Britain would fit into it more than six times.

D Tropical rainforests

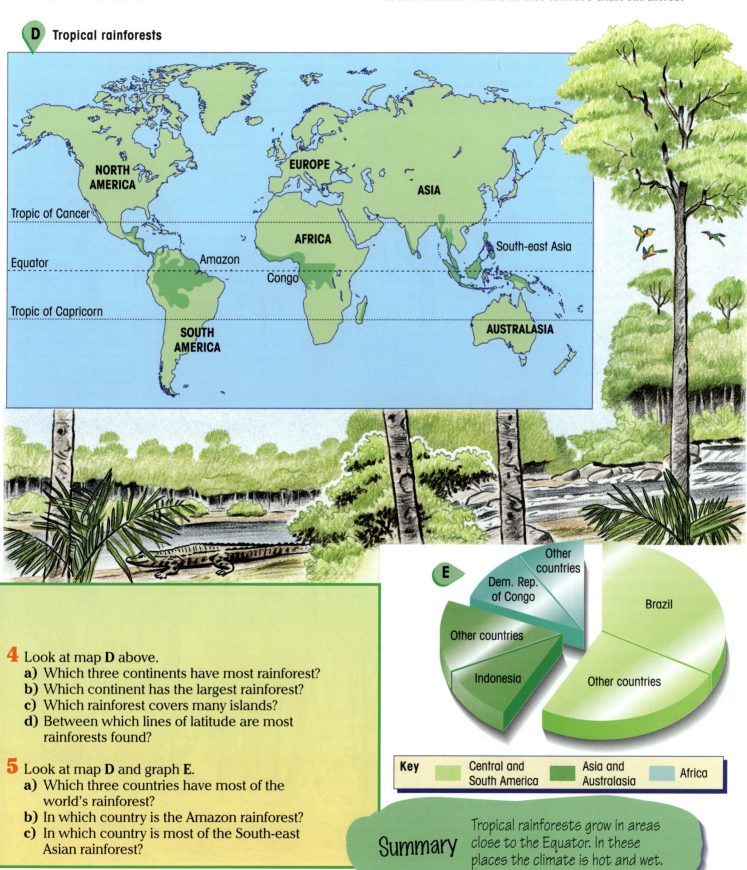

4 Look at map **D** above.
  a) Which three continents have most rainforest?
  b) Which continent has the largest rainforest?
  c) Which rainforest covers many islands?
  d) Between which lines of latitude are most rainforests found?

5 Look at map **D** and graph **E**.
  a) Which three countries have most of the world's rainforest?
  b) In which country is the Amazon rainforest?
  c) In which country is most of the South-east Asian rainforest?

Key

| Central and South America | Asia and Australasia | Africa |

Summary   Tropical rainforests grow in areas close to the Equator. In these places the climate is hot and wet.

117

What are tropical rainforests like?

The drawing below shows what it is like in the tropical rainforests. Notice that there are three separate layers. The lowest is the forest floor. Above this is a layer of mainly new trees. The top layer is the canopy which is like an umbrella sheltering the forest below. Within these three layers live many thousands of different animals, birds and insects.

- The highest trees form a **canopy** over the forest.
- They protect the lower layers from wind and rain.
- Birds and climbing animals like monkeys live here.

1 The tallest trees get most sunlight. They are called **emergents**.

2 Tree trunks are straight and have few branches.

3 New trees grow quickly upwards, looking for sunlight.

4 Leaves have **drip tips** so that rain can drain off easily.

5 The forest is **evergreen**. This is because plants grow all through the year.

6 Some shrubs and bushes grow on the forest floor.

7 Dead leaves quickly rot away to make new soil.

- The forest floor is dark and steamy.
- Lack of sunlight makes the vegetation thinner here.
- This is the home of animals like jaguars and deer.

Activities

This quiz covers all of this chapter so far. The information that you need is on pages 114 to 118.

1 Start at the top left-hand box and follow the arrows around the quiz. Answer **true** or **false** to each statement. Write down the letters found in each box as you go along.
Answer like this: **1 = true = R**

2 Write out the **true** letters. Then write out the **false** letters. They should spell out words that have a link with tropical rainforests.

3 Now write out the **true** statements.

Start here

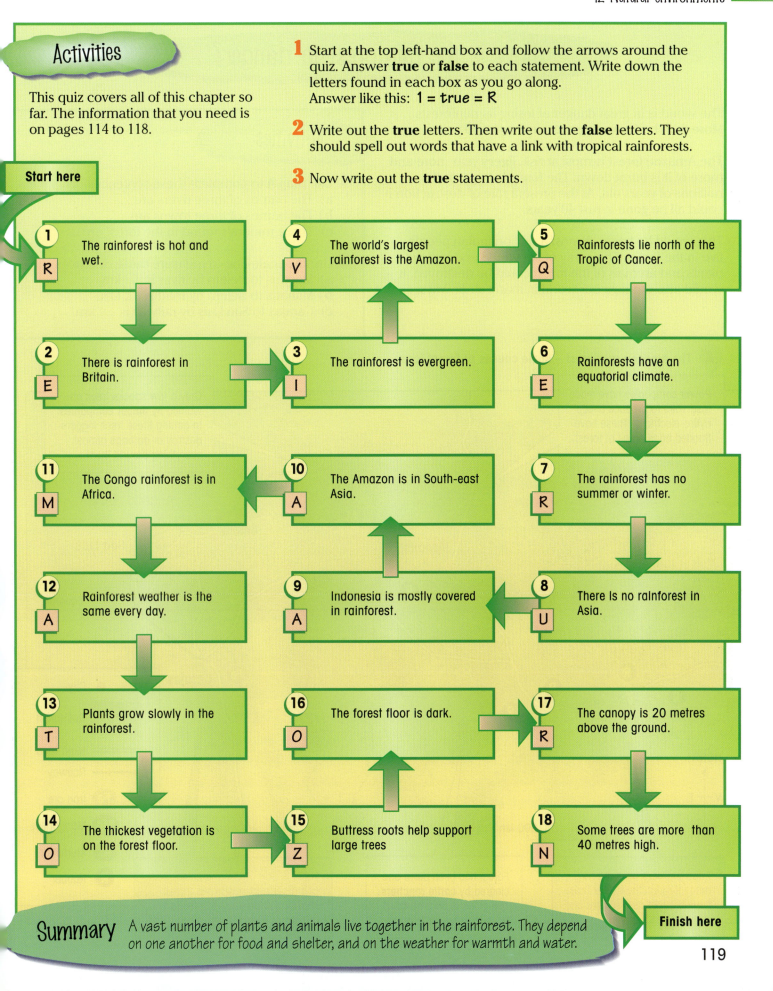

1 R	The rainforest is hot and wet.
2 E	There is rainforest in Britain.
3 I	The rainforest is evergreen.
4 V	The world's largest rainforest is the Amazon.
5 Q	Rainforests lie north of the Tropic of Cancer.
6 E	Rainforests have an equatorial climate.
7 R	The rainforest has no summer or winter.
8 U	There Is no rainforest in Asia.
9 A	Indonesia is mostly covered in rainforest.
10 A	The Amazon is in South-east Asia.
11 M	The Congo rainforest is in Africa.
12 A	Rainforest weather is the same every day.
13 T	Plants grow slowly in the rainforest.
14 O	The thickest vegetation is on the forest floor.
15 Z	Buttress roots help support large trees
16 O	The forest floor is dark.
17 R	The canopy is 20 metres above the ground.
18 N	Some trees are more than 40 metres high.

Finish here

Summary A vast number of plants and animals live together in the rainforest. They depend on one another for food and shelter, and on the weather for warmth and water.

How is the rainforest in danger?

The world is in great danger of losing its rainforests. More than half have been lost in the last 50 years.

The Amazon forest is most at risk. Every year more and more of it is burnt down. The forest is huge, and millions of years old. At the present rate of destruction it could all be gone in just 40 years.

This would be tragic. Almost a million Indian people live in the forest. Their way of life would end and the plants and animals of the forest could be destroyed. It would also damage our world in many other ways.

Activities

1 Use map **A** to complete these sentences.
 a) The names of three rivers are ......
 b) The names of three towns are ......
 c) Three minerals found in the forest are ......

2 Use the scale-line to measure these distances.
 a) Manaus to Belem by river is ..... km.
 b) Manaus to Belem by road is ..... km.
 c) Carajas to São Luis by railway is ..... km.

A **The Amazon rainforest – some causes of forest loss**

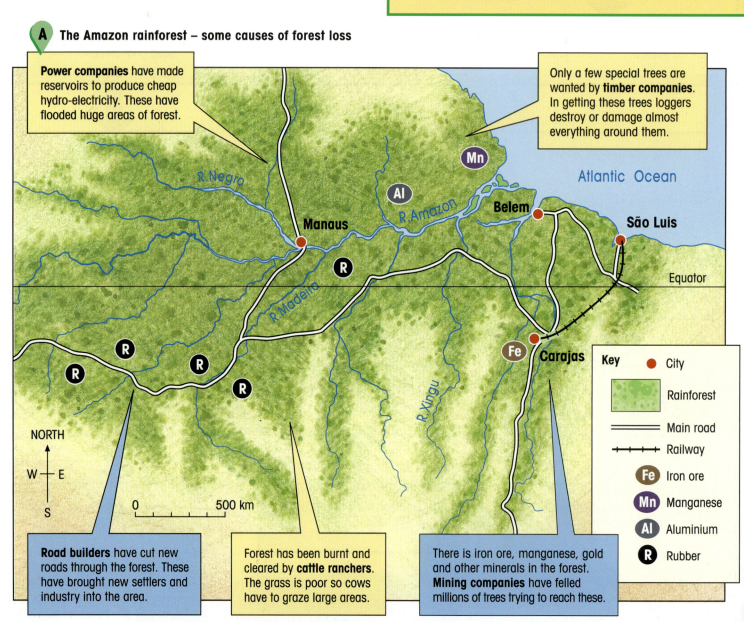

Power companies have made reservoirs to produce cheap hydro-electricity. These have flooded huge areas of forest.

Only a few special trees are wanted by **timber companies**. In getting these trees loggers destroy or damage almost everything around them.

Atlantic Ocean

R.Negro

R.Amazon

Manaus

Belem

São Luis

Equator

R.Madeira

R.Xingu

Carajas

NORTH

W — E

S

0   500 km

Road builders have cut new roads through the forest. These have brought new settlers and industry into the area.

Forest has been burnt and cleared by **cattle ranchers**. The grass is poor so cows have to graze large areas.

There is iron ore, manganese, gold and other minerals in the forest. **Mining companies** have felled millions of trees trying to reach these.

Key
- ● City
- Rainforest
- Main road
- +++ Railway
- **Fe** Iron ore
- **Mn** Manganese
- **Al** Aluminium
- **R** Rubber

3 Use the information on map **A** for this activity. Name five groups or organisations that have helped cause a loss of rainforest.

4 Make a copy of table **B**. Sort the statements from drawing **C** into the correct columns. You need only write the number. The first one has been done for you.

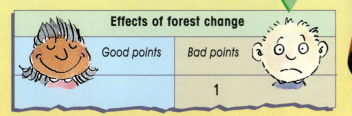

B

Effects of forest change		
	Good points	Bad points
		1

5 Drawing **C** will help you with this activity. Copy and complete the sentences below.

We are against forest clearance because ......

We want the forest left as it is because ......

Brazil needs mining because ......

Kayapo Indian **A European tourist** **Mine owner**

Summary There have been many changes to the Amazon rainforest. These have brought benefits but have also caused problems.

C Changes to the Amazon rainforest – some effects

1 The Indian way of life has had to change

2 Cheap power helps run new industries

3 Improved transport is good for the country

4 Many plants and animals have been lost

5 Clearing the forest ruins the soil for ever

6 Mining provides people with jobs

7 Industry has poisoned some rivers

8 Many Indian villages have been flooded

9 Developing the forest helps Brazil get richer

10 Many forest products are sold abroad. This brings in money.

11 Losing the rainforest may change world climate

Where do volcanoes and earthquakes happen?

Earthquakes and **volcanic eruptions** are the most spectacular and dangerous of all **natural hazards**. They happen all the time and scientists continuously record and measure them. We only hear of the ones that do most damage, but in 2002, for example, over 840 big earthquakes and 350 different volcanic eruptions were recorded.

Some people think that earthquakes and volcanic eruptions can happen anywhere. This is not the case. Look carefully at map **D**. You will see that most volcanoes and earthquakes occur in the same places. They are usually found in long narrow belts across the Earth's surface. One belt circles the Pacific Ocean. This is called 'The Ring of Fire'.

A　The eruption of Mount Pinatubo

Activities

B

1 Name the volcano or earthquake for each of the following. The spaces for the letters will help you.

  a) Japanese earthquake in 1995
  b) 1976 earthquake in Asia
  c) North American earthquake
  d) Volcano on Pacific Ocean island
  e) Volcano on Indian Ocean island
  f) Central American earthquake
  g) 1998 West Indies volcano
  h) 1976 earthquake in Asia
  i) Famous North American earthquake

3 Make a simple sketch of photo **A**. Add these labels.
- Steep sides
- Cone shape
- Eruption of ash and steam
- Farmland covered in ash
- Volcano

2 Of the following statements, five are correct. Put the correct ones into a copy of star diagram **C**.

C

Where volcanoes and earthquakes are found

Earthquakes and volcanoes are found …

- in the same places
- only in the oceans
- in narrow belts
- all over the world
- along the west coast of the Americas
- off the east coast of Asia
- circling the Pacific Ocean
- on American east coast
- mainly in Africa

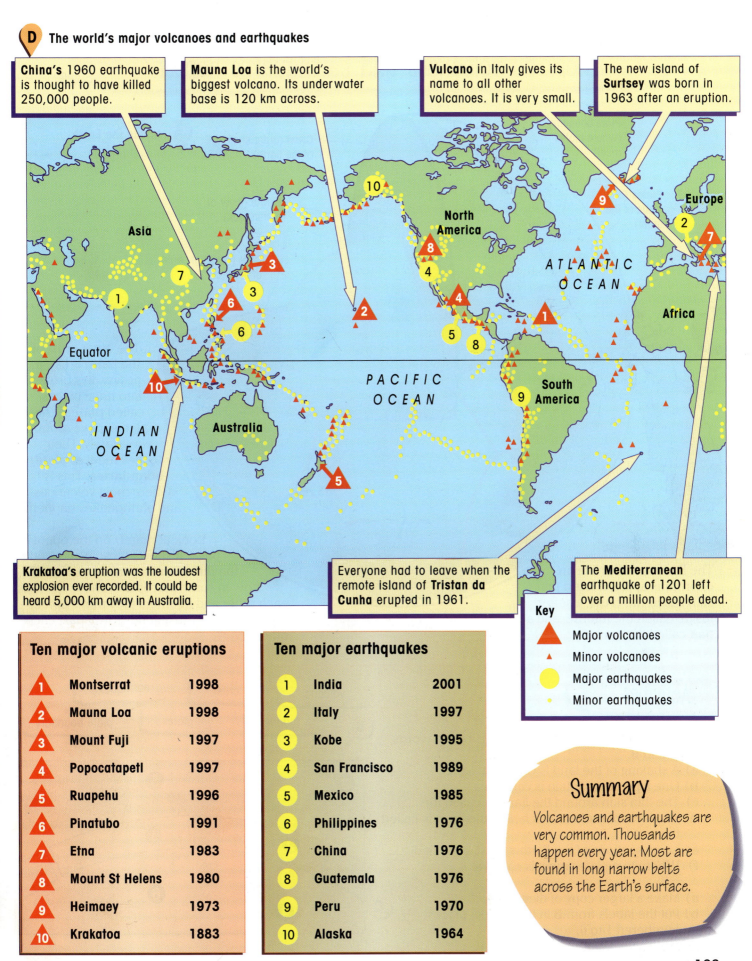

China's 1960 earthquake is thought to have killed 250,000 people.

Mauna Loa is the world's biggest volcano. Its under water base is 120 km across.

Vulcano in Italy gives its name to all other volcanoes. It is very small.

The new island of **Surtsey** was born in 1963 after an eruption.

Krakatoa's eruption was the loudest explosion ever recorded. It could be heard 5,000 km away in Australia.

Everyone had to leave when the remote island of **Tristan da Cunha** erupted in 1961.

The **Mediterranean** earthquake of 1201 left over a million people dead.

Asia
North America
ATLANTIC OCEAN
Europe
Africa
Equator
PACIFIC OCEAN
South America
INDIAN OCEAN
Australia

Key

▲	Major volcanoes
▴	Minor volcanoes
●	Major earthquakes
·	Minor earthquakes

Ten major volcanic eruptions

1	Montserrat	1998
2	Mauna Loa	1998
3	Mount Fuji	1997
4	Popocatapetl	1997
5	Ruapehu	1996
6	Pinatubo	1991
7	Etna	1983
8	Mount St Helens	1980
9	Heimaey	1973
10	Krakatoa	1883

Ten major earthquakes

1	India	2001
2	Italy	1997
3	Kobe	1995
4	San Francisco	1989
5	Mexico	1985
6	Philippines	1976
7	China	1976
8	Guatemala	1976
9	Peru	1970
10	Alaska	1964

Summary

Volcanoes and earthquakes are very common. Thousands happen every year. Most are found in long narrow belts across the Earth's surface.

How do volcanoes and earthquakes happen?

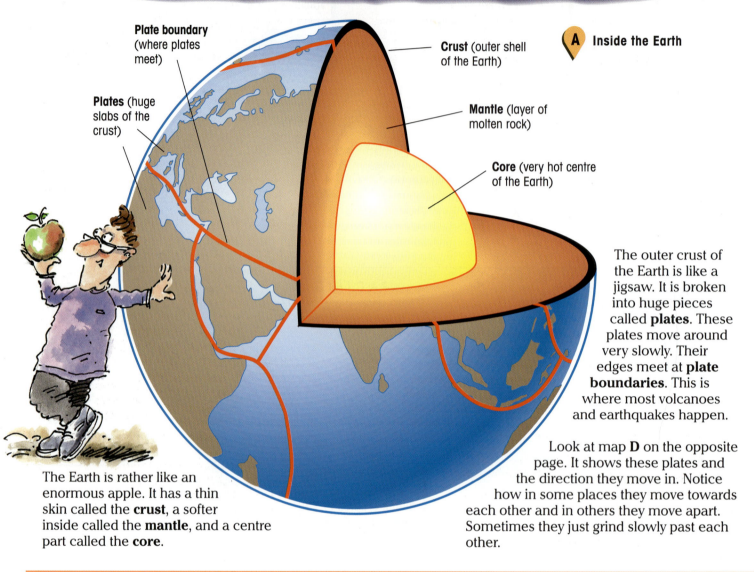

Plate boundary (where plates meet)

Plates (huge slabs of the crust)

Crust (outer shell of the Earth)

A Inside the Earth

Mantle (layer of molten rock)

Core (very hot centre of the Earth)

The outer crust of the Earth is like a jigsaw. It is broken into huge pieces called **plates**. These plates move around very slowly. Their edges meet at **plate boundaries**. This is where most volcanoes and earthquakes happen.

Look at map **D** on the opposite page. It shows these plates and the direction they move in. Notice how in some places they move towards each other and in others they move apart. Sometimes they just grind slowly past each other.

The Earth is rather like an enormous apple. It has a thin skin called the **crust**, a softer inside called the **mantle**, and a centre part called the **core**.

Activities

B volcano   crust   earthquake   mantle   plates   plate boundary

1 Complete the following sentences using the words shown in **B**.
  a) A shaking of the land is called an ......
  b) One type of mountain is called a ......
  c) The thin skin around the Earth is called the ......
  d) The layer of molten rock below the crust is called the ......
  e) Large sections of the Earth's crust are called ......
  f) Where two plates meet is called a ......

2 **a)** Make a larger copy of diagram **C**.
  b) Put the labels from **B** in the correct places numbered 1 to 6.

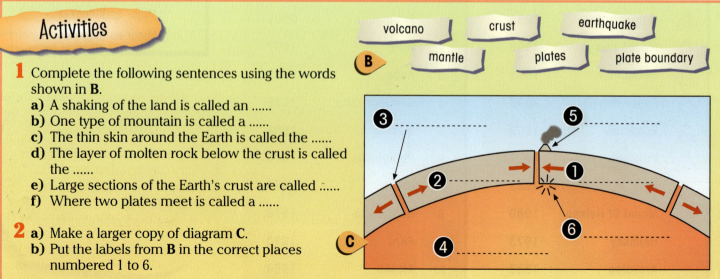

D The jigsaw of plates

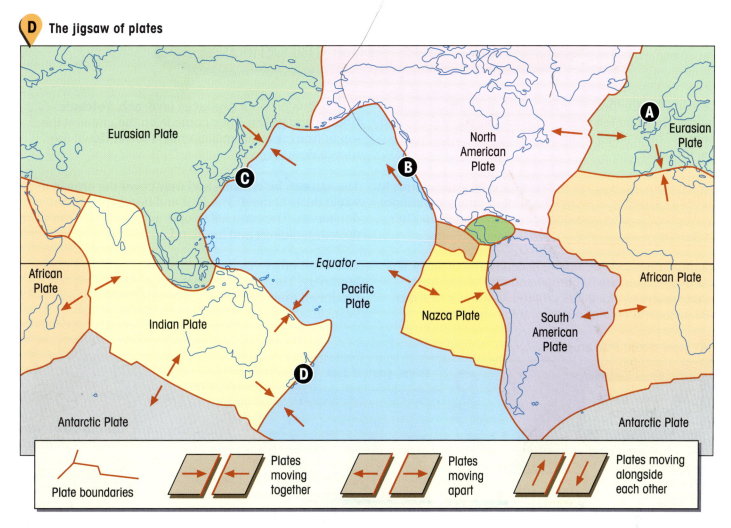

Where plates meet, the land itself may shake. This is called an **earthquake**. Earthquakes are caused by movements deep below the surface. They last only a few seconds but can be very damaging. The fires that followed the 1906 earthquake in San Francisco destroyed almost all of the city.

Most volcanoes may be found where plates either come together or move apart. At these places, the Earth's crust is weak, and red-hot molten rock underneath the crust can force its way upwards. On reaching the surface it **erupts** to form a volcano.

3 Look carefully at map **D**.
   a) On which plate is Britain (A)?
   b) Which two plates meet near San Francisco (B)?
   c) Which two plates meet near Japan (C)?
   d) Which two plates meet near New Zealand (D)?

4 Look at map **D** and complete these sentences. Choose from **moving apart**, **moving together** or **moving alongside each other**.
   a) The plates near San Francisco (B) are ......
   b) The plates near Japan (C) are ......
   c) The plates near New Zealand (D) are ......

5 Copy and complete the following sentences.

The Earth's crust is made up of several .... Each plate moves very s...... in a d...... direction. Most v...... and e...... happen on plate b...... .

Summary

The Earth's crust is made up of several plates that move about very slowly. Volcanoes and earthquakes are most likely to occur in areas where the plates meet.

Mount Etna: What happened?

Late in 1991 the people living near Mount Etna began to worry. They had felt many small earthquakes and could hear the occasional rumbling noise from deep inside the mountain.

Steam from the main crater was causing great clouds to develop. There was sometimes heavy rain with thunder and lightning. Etna was preparing itself for yet another eruption!

Mount Etna is located on the Italian island of Sicily. It is the biggest volcano in Europe and one of the most **active** in the world. It has erupted 46 times in the last 100 years and continuously rumbles and steams.

When Etna erupts it produces **lava**, **ash**, **volcanic bombs** and **gases**. They come from the crater at the top or from several smaller craters lower down the mountainside.

The ash can be choking and may cover the area in a white dusty blanket. The lava and bombs are more dangerous. They can kill people and animals. They also destroy buildings and farmland.

Like most other volcanoes, Etna is located on a plate boundary. The boundary that runs through Italy has produced many volcanoes, including the famous Vesuvius. Earthquakes are also common here.

A **How Mount Etna erupts**

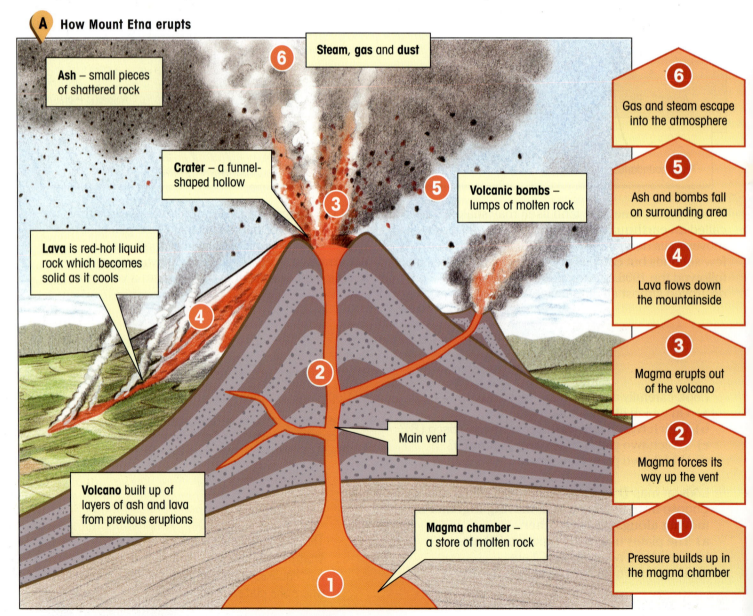

Steam, gas and **dust**

Ash – small pieces of shattered rock

Crater – a funnel-shaped hollow

Volcanic bombs – lumps of molten rock

Lava is red-hot liquid rock which becomes solid as it cools

Main vent

Volcano built up of layers of ash and lava from previous eruptions

Magma chamber – a store of molten rock

6 Gas and steam escape into the atmosphere

5 Ash and bombs fall on surrounding area

4 Lava flows down the mountainside

3 Magma erupts out of the volcano

2 Magma forces its way up the vent

1 Pressure builds up in the magma chamber

B Location of Mount Etna

Key
▲ Volcanoes
High ground
• Main towns
— Plate boundary
⇨ Plate movement

C Mount Etna and some main lava flows

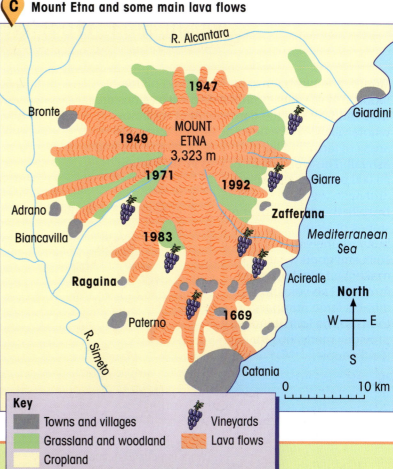

Key
Towns and villages
Grassland and woodland
Cropland
Vineyards
Lava flows

Activities

1 Look at drawing **D** below. Match each of the following with a letter from the drawing. Drawing **A** will help you.
Answer like this: **A = Volcano erupts**

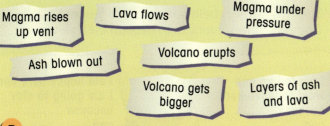

Magma rises up vent

Lava flows

Magma under pressure

Ash blown out

Volcano erupts

Volcano gets bigger

Layers of ash and lava

2 Look at map **B**.
a) Name four volcanoes in Italy.
b) Which large town is nearest to Mount Etna?
c) Which large town is nearest to Vesuvius?
d) Which two plates meet over Italy?
e) Are the plates moving apart or towards each other?

3 Look at map **C**.
a) Which village was threatened by the 1983 lava flow?
b) Which village was threatened by the 1992 lava flow?
c) What is the length of the 1992 lava flow?
d) What is the length of the longest lava flow?

D How a volcano grows

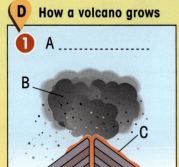

① A ....

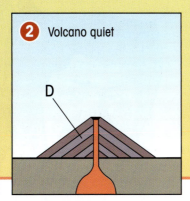

② Volcano quiet

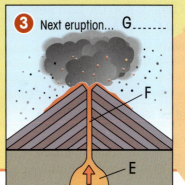

③ Next eruption... G ....

Summary

Volcanoes are openings in the ground where molten rock, ash and gases force their way to the surface.

127

Mount Etna: What were the effects?

Mount Etna has been erupting on and off for thousands of years. Sometimes the eruptions are small and cause little damage. At other times whole villages have been destroyed and large areas of farmland laid to waste by lava flows and ash fall. The worst disaster was in 1669 when 20,000 people were killed.

Despite the danger, over one million people live on the slopes of Mount Etna. This is mainly because the very rich volcanic soils and good weather there make it an ideal place for farming. The volcano also attracts large numbers of tourists. The tourist industry provides many jobs for local people.

A

Mount Etna lava flow

Activities

Work in pairs or a small group for these activities. This will help you share other people's views and ideas.

1 Six of the ten words below help describe photo **A**. Put them into a sentence.

- dangerous
- red-hot lava
- quickly
- safe
- low
- flat
- river
- quiet
- downhill
- moving

2 Look at the information below drawing **C** opposite. Six of the statements are **good news**. Write them out.

3 Make a copy of table **B** below. Sort the **bad news** statements from drawing **C** into the correct columns. You need only write the number for each one. Two have been done for you.

4 Look at drawing **D**. Name six towns or villages affected by Mount Etna eruptions.

5 The two farmers below live near to Mount Etna. Complete the sentences to explain their views.

I am fed up and want to leave here because .... and ....

I am happy here and I am going to stay because .... and ....

B

Some problems caused by Mount Etna eruptions		
Farming	Tourism	Others
①	③	

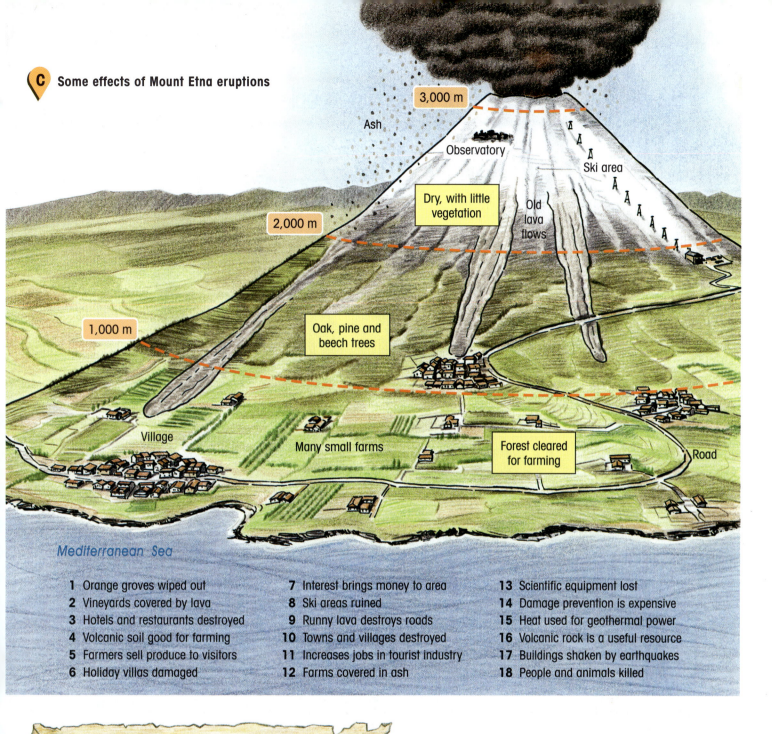

C Some effects of Mount Etna eruptions

3,000 m

Ash

Observatory

Ski area

Dry, with little vegetation

Old lava flows

2,000 m

1,000 m

Oak, pine and beech trees

Village

Many small farms

Forest cleared for farming

Road

Mediterranean Sea

1 Orange groves wiped out	**7** Interest brings money to area	**13** Scientific equipment lost
2 Vineyards covered by lava	**8** Ski areas ruined	**14** Damage prevention is expensive
3 Hotels and restaurants destroyed	**9** Runny lava destroys roads	**15** Heat used for geothermal power
4 Volcanic soil good for farming	**10** Towns and villages destroyed	**16** Volcanic rock is a useful resource
5 Farmers sell produce to visitors	**11** Increases jobs in tourist industry	**17** Buildings shaken by earthquakes
6 Holiday villas damaged	**12** Farms covered in ash	**18** People and animals killed

SOME ETNA ERUPTIONS **D**

693 BC – first recorded eruption
1669 – town of Catania destroyed
1792 – Zafferana hit by lava flow
1908 – town of Messina destroyed
1928 – lava covers village of Mascali
1971 – summit observatory wrecked
1978 – lava partly destroys Fornazzo
1979 – nine tourists killed
1983 – Sapienza overcome by lava
1984 – Zafferana church cracks in half
1992 – eruptions continue for four months
2002 – several villages evacuated

Summary

Volcanoes like Mount Etna are dangerous and can cause much damage to property and the surroundings. They can also bring benefits to the local area.

Mount Etna: How did people respond?

People in the Mount Etna area are well used to their volcano erupting. They can never stop the eruptions but have learned ways of reducing the damage and danger that the eruptions cause.

Zafferana is a farming village 10 km from the summit of Mount Etna. It was badly hit by lava in 1792, then enjoyed 200 years without damage. Late in 1991 the village was once again threatened. This time the eruption lasted four months.

A

Scientists continually monitor small earthquakes. This helps them forecast when the next eruption might occur.

Emergency services are trained and ready for an eruption.

Their first aim is to protect human life. This may mean moving people out of a danger area.

They also try to reduce the damage done to property and farmland.

B Storyboard of an eruption: Zafferana

1 **14 December 1991**

Major eruption. Millions of tonnes of lava spill down mountainside.

2 **January 1992**

Lava flows into old crater. Army builds dam to trap it there.

That should stop it.

3 **Early April 1992**

Lava overflows crater and threatens village.

4 **12 April 1992**

Italian Army use dynamite to slow lava flow.

That's had no effect at all.

5 **14 April 1992**

United States Army drop 2-tonne concrete blocks to stop lava.

The blocks are just floating away.

6 **15 April 1992**

Vineyards are destroyed on edge of Zafferana.

Our life's work is all gone.

7 **17 April 1992**

Lava destroys houses and farm buildings.

Another 500 metres and we've lost the village.

8 **23 April 1992**

Strengthened dams above village divert lava.

Safe at last. It's gone round us.

Activities

1 a) When did the eruption start?
b) When was the village first threatened?
c) On what dates were army teams brought in?
d) When was Zafferana finally declared safe?

2 a) How close to the village did the lava get?
b) What three ways were tried to stop the lava?
c) Why was building dams with bulldozers difficult?
d) What method of protection finally saved the village?

3 Drawing **C** shows how the damage and danger caused by an eruption may be reduced. Write out the six points of the plan in the order you think they should happen.

C

Mt Etna Disaster Plan

- Re-building started
- Emergency services plan and train
- Scientists monitor earthquakes
- Warning given of eruption
- Property protected
- People moved out of area

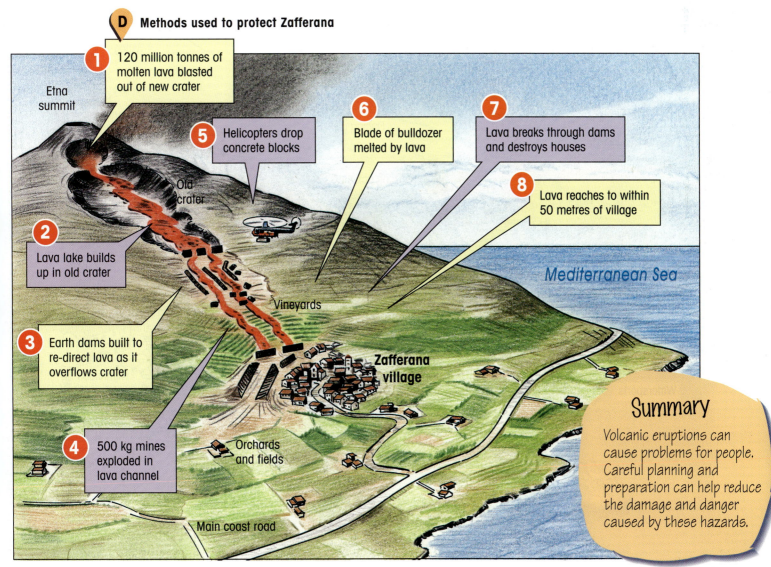

D Methods used to protect Zafferana

1 120 million tonnes of molten lava blasted out of new crater

Etna summit

Old crater

5 Helicopters drop concrete blocks

6 Blade of bulldozer melted by lava

7 Lava breaks through dams and destroys houses

8 Lava reaches to within 50 metres of village

2 Lava lake builds up in old crater

Mediterranean Sea

3 Earth dams built to re-direct lava as it overflows crater

Vineyards

Zafferana village

4 500 kg mines exploded in lava channel

Orchards and fields

Main coast road

Summary

Volcanic eruptions can cause problems for people. Careful planning and preparation can help reduce the damage and danger caused by these hazards.

131

14 Tourism

What is the tourist industry?

Tourists are people who travel to places for pleasure. The tourist industry looks after the needs of these people. First it helps them get to their destination. Then it helps them relax and enjoy themselves once they are there.

Tourism is the world's largest industry. It employs over 200 million people worldwide and is still growing. It is an example of a **tertiary industry**.

There are many different jobs in tourism. They include travel agents, airline pilots, hotel managers, and waiters. The photos on the next page show some others. Can you think of any more?

Tertiary industries provide a service. People who give help to others, such as teachers, nurses and shop assistants, are part of this industry.

Nowadays, most holiday resorts provide a variety of activities for people to do. Drawing **A** shows some of these.

A

Skiing

Jeep trips

Safari park visits

Mountain biking

Historic visits

Fishing

2

6

Sporting activities

Boat trips

Quad biking

5

Walking

Relaxing

Shopping

3

Nightclubs

1

Watersports

Sunbathing

4

Sailing

Activities

1 Look at drawing **A**. List the five activities you would most like to do. Give your favourite first.

2 Write a diary for your first day on holiday. Try to have at least eight entries.
You could start like this:

Monday

9.00 - Get up.
9.30 - Breakfast at hotel.
10.30 - have a wank

3 Match the numbers on drawing **A** with the following resort features.
Answer like this: **1 = Restaurant**

- Airport
- Hotel
- Restaurant
- Tourist attraction
- Cruise boat
- Water park

4 Match photos **B** to **G** with the following jobs.
Answer like this: **B = Baggage handler**

- Lifeguard
- Chef
- Entertainers
- Baggage handler
- Tour guide
- Receptionist

5 Make a larger copy of table **H**. Complete the table as follows.
a) List the resort features from activity 3.
b) Match a job from activity 4 to each feature.
c) Try to add two more jobs for each feature.
The first one has been started for you.

H

Number	Resort feature	Blow Jobs
1	Restaurant	Waiter
2		
3		

Summary

Tourism provides more jobs worldwide than any other industry. It is an example of a service, or tertiary, industry.

133

What benefits does tourism bring?

Majorca is one of the Balearic Islands. It lies just off the coast of Spain in the Mediterranean Sea. Just 40 years ago Spain was one of the poorest countries in Europe and Majorca one of its poorest regions.

Today, things are very different. Spain is now wealthy and Majorca is no longer poor. The main reason for this change is tourism.

For many people, Majorca is the perfect holiday resort. There is beautiful scenery, guaranteed summer sunshine, safe beaches for swimming and plenty of things to do. Over 7 million tourists visit the island each year.

For most people in Majorca, tourism has been good news. It has brought in money, helped create jobs and improved **standards of living**. Some of the benefits that the tourist industry can bring to an area are shown in drawings **B** and **C**.

Some benefits of tourism

Tourists bring millions of pounds into Majorca every year.

There is a much greater demand for locally produced food. This has helped the farmers.

Money from tourism has been spent on improving our hospitals, schools and roads.

The island looks much better now. Old buildings have been repaired and the whole place tidied up.

There are more things for us to do now. We can use the amenities provided for tourists.

There are plenty of tourist jobs available. Many are in hotels and restaurants.

Our way of life used to be very old-fashioned. Tourism has helped us modernise.

Tourism has brought new ideas to the island. It is more interesting to live here now.

134

C **Storyboard: A farming family discuss their future**

Activities

D

Local farmer

Tourism has been good for me because … and …

Two school children aged 12 and 16

Tourism has been good for us because … and …

1 Match the letters on photo **A** with the following resort features.

Answer like this: **A = Restaurants and cafés.**

- Attractive scenery
- Clean, sandy beach
- Restaurants and cafés
- Hot, sunny weather
- Calm, warm sea
- Modern hotels

2 Write a paragraph to describe photo **A**. Include the features from activity 1.

3 The people in drawing **D** live in Majorca. Complete the speech bubbles to describe how they have benefited from tourism.

Summary

Tourism can bring many benefits. It can increase wealth, help create jobs and improve facilities for local people.

Tourism – what are the problems ...

Tourism has brought many benefits to Majorca but it has also caused problems.

Many islanders worry about the noise, litter, violence and drunkenness that has become common in some places. They also worry about the effects of tourism on Spanish traditions and their local way of life.

They argue that most of the jobs in the tourist industry are unskilled and poorly paid. Many are also seasonal. This means there is no work and no money coming in for much of the year.

Some other problems caused by the growth of tourism in Majorca are shown below.

A

PROBLEMS

1 Overcrowding of popular resorts made the area less attractive to visitors.

2 Rowdiness and bad behaviour of some tourists caused major problems.

3 Many tourist buildings from the 1960s were ugly and spoilt the landscape.

4 Traffic congestion became a serious problem as the use of hire cars increased.

5 Beaches became polluted by sewage discharged from hotels and boats into the sea.

6 Large areas of farmland and attractive countryside have been lost to tourist developments.

Activities

B

1 Make a larger copy of diagram B. Complete the diagram by putting the following statements into the correct boxes.

Attractions of resort spoilt

Resort filled with tourists

Tourists go elsewhere

Rush to build new facilities

Cheap holidays available

↓

↓

↓

Lack of planning and control

↓

↓

... and possible solutions?

In the 1990s the government of Majorca became worried about a fall in tourist numbers. It realised that tourism had spoilt the island and many visitors were choosing to go elsewhere.

The government acted quickly and brought out a plan for the future. The three main points of the plan are shown in drawing **C**.

C

Plan for the future

1 Try to attract a 'better type' of tourist

2 Protect the natural beauty of the island

3 Improve the existing tourist facilities

D

SOLUTIONS

7 A third of the island has been made a nature reserve to protect it from development.

8 New attractions are being introduced to spread tourists more evenly around the island.

9 New motorways have been built around Palma, the main town.

10 Many unsightly hotels have been knocked down. New ones have to be built to very high standards.

11 Strict regulations have been introduced to improve waste disposal.

12 Majorca has gone upmarket in an attempt to attract wealthier, better behaved tourists.

2 Make a copy of table **E**.
  a) Use drawing **A** to complete the 'Problem' column.
  b) Use drawing **D** to complete the 'Solution' column.
You need only write in the number. The first one has been done for you.

3 a) Describe the problems shown in photo **A**.
  b) Suggest what could be done to reduce these problems.

E

Feature	Problem	Solution
Buildings	3	10
Traffic		
Countryside		
Beaches		
Behaviour		
Overcrowding		

Summary

Tourism can cause problems for people and spoil the environment. Care is needed in planning and managing tourist environments.

Where shall we go on holiday?

We all like holidays. It's a time when we can relax and enjoy ourselves. Nowadays there is a wider choice of holidays available then ever before. Travel is easier and cheaper, and people have longer holidays than in the past.

So how do we choose a holiday? There are a few things we should consider. Look at drawing **A** which shows some questions to think about.

Given a choice, where in the world would you like to go and what would you like to do? The places shown below may give you some ideas.

What do you want to do?

Where do you want to go?

When do you want to go?

How much do you want to spend?

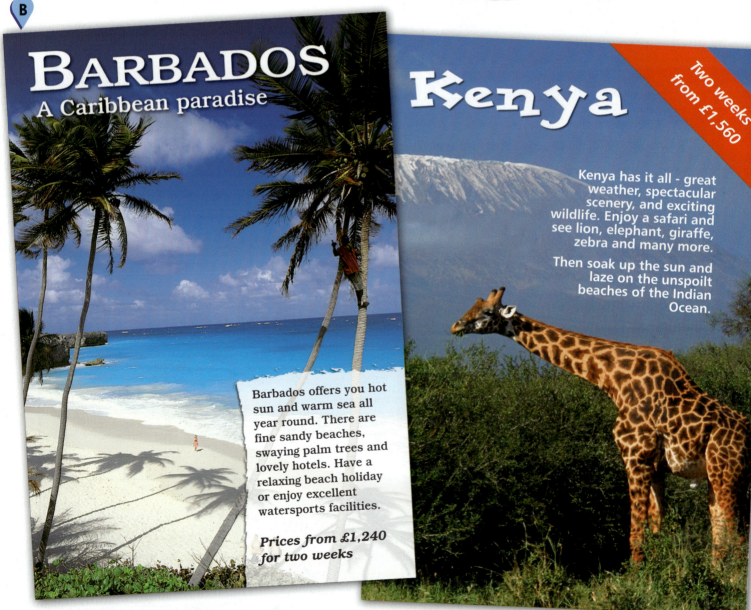

BARBADOS
A Caribbean paradise

Barbados offers you hot sun and warm sea all year round. There are fine sandy beaches, swaying palm trees and lovely hotels. Have a relaxing beach holiday or enjoy excellent watersports facilities.

Prices from £1,240 for two weeks

Kenya

Two weeks from £1,560

Kenya has it all - great weather, spectacular scenery, and exciting wildlife. Enjoy a safari and see lion, elephant, giraffe, zebra and many more.

Then soak up the sun and laze on the unspoilt beaches of the Indian Ocean.

Activities

1 Complete these sentences.
a) The most expensive holiday is ...
b) The two cheapest holidays are ...
c) The holidays with sports activities are ...
d) The holidays with the best weather are ...

2 List the attractions of Kenya as a holiday destination. Try to give at least four.

3 Look at the people shown in drawing **C**. Choose the most suitable holiday for them. Give reasons for your choice.

4 Where would you most like to go on holiday? You can choose from anywhere in the world. Give reasons for your choice.

> We would like a winter holiday where it is quiet and warm.

> We've got three kids. We need somewhere with plenty for them to do and where we can relax.

C

A retired couple · A young family

Florida

Glorious sunshine and hot all year... the wonderful world of Disney and the Epcot Center... Universal Studios and Wet 'n' Wild... fun and entertainment for all the family. Then chill out on the beach and maybe swim with the dolphins.

Two weeks from £740 per person

Ski Zermatt

Come to Switzerland's top ski resort. See the famous Matterhorn and use some of Europe's best winter sports facilities. Enjoy the delights of a friendly and interesting alpine village.

Two weeks from £620

Summary

Cheaper and quicker travel has made it possible to holiday almost anywhere in the world. Deciding where to go needs careful thought.

How can we make notes from photos?

Photos can show a lot of information. In geography we need to learn ways of simplifying that information so that we can look at the things we are most interested in.

Writing short notes or summaries can help us do this. A **summary** is a brief account that gives only the main points of something.

Making a summary can best be done in three easy steps. These are shown in drawings **A** and **B** below.

A **summary** is a short piece of writing that has only relevant information. Writing down relevant information is called **summarising**.

A

Look  Choose  Write

 B

1. a) **Look** at the title for information about what the photo shows.
   b) **Look** at all of the photo, not just part of it. What does it show?
   c) **Look** for the main feature or features. What are those features like?

2. a) **Choose** the features that are relevant to your study.
   b) **Choose** which of those features are the most important and which you want to use.

3. a) **Write** a short sentence to describe what the photo shows.
   b) **Write** short sentences to describe each of the features that are important to your study.
   c) **Write** a brief sentence to summarise what you have written.

Derwentwater in the Lake District

C The Dolomites, northern Italy

D Benidorm, Spain

Activities

1 Look at photo **B**. Of the seven sentences below, five are correct. Write out the correct ones.
- The photo shows Derwentwater.
- The lake is surrounded by mountains.
- The mountains are covered in forest.
- The island is covered in woodland.
- There are several boats on the lake.
- There is a beach all around the lake.
- The area is popular with tourists.

2 Look at photo **C**. Match the following beginnings with the correct endings.

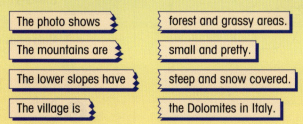

The photo shows	forest and grassy areas.
The mountains are	small and pretty.
The lower slopes have	steep and snow covered.
The village is	the Dolomites in Italy.

3 Look at photo **D**. Match the letters on the photo with the words below.

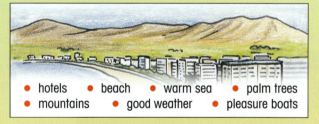

- hotels
- beach
- warm sea
- palm trees
- mountains
- good weather
- pleasure boats

4 Write a summary of photo **D**. Use the following sentence beginnings.
- The photo shows ...
- The beach is ...
- The hotels are ...
- The mountains are ...
- Benidorm is ...

Summary

To write a summary of a photo, you need to look carefully at the photo, choose the important features, and write a short sentence on each.

What are Italy's main features?

A

B The Italian lakes

Milan

Turin

River Po

Genoa

Florence

R. Arno

B

D Venice

A L P S

A P E N N I N E S

R. Tiber

Rome

Sardinia

Naples

E

Bari

Mt Vesuvius

C

Mediterranean Sea

Palermo

Mt Etna

Sicily

The Amalfi coast near Naples

C

Key

◇	Highland
	Lowland
●	Main cities
🌋	Volcano
C	Photo location

North
W — E
S

0   200 km

All of us have heard of Italy. It is one of Europe's best-known countries. But what does Italy make you think of? Football, food, fast cars and fashions perhaps? Cities like Rome, Milan and Naples, with their great history and noisy, excitable people? Or spectacular mountain scenery, rocky coastlines and hot dry summers?

What does Italy mean to you? Try to think of ten things that come to mind.

In fact, like most countries, Italy is a land of contrasts and variety. There are high snow-covered mountains in the north and hot, dry plains in the south. There are huge factories and the latest high-tech industries in some places, and simple peasant farming in others. Some people are very rich and some people very poor. All in all, Italy is a most interesting and varied country.

D The city of Venice

E

A hill village in the Apennines

Activities

1 Use map **A** to complete these sentences.
   a) The names of two islands are ......
   b) The names of two mountain areas are ......
   c) The names of two volcanoes are ......
   d) The names of two rivers are ......
   e) The names of two inland towns are ......

2 Use chart **F** below to measure these distances. The first one has been done for you.
   a) Florence to Rome = **277 km**
   b) Turin to Venice =
   c) Milan to Palermo =
   d) Bari to Rome =
   e) Genoa to Naples =

Bari

720	Florence							
944	227	Genoa						
878	298	120	Milan					
261	490	714	785	Naples				
692	1211	1435	1506	734	Palermo			
449	277	501	572	219	940	Rome		
997	395	170	140	882	1593	669	Turin	
760	254	398	267	741	1462	523	390	Venice

F

3 a) Write a sentence to describe each of the photos **B**, **C**, **D** and **E**. The words below will help you.
   b) Give each description a heading.

B	lake – mountains – village
C	coastline – steep – rocky
D	city – canals – attractive buildings
E	village – hills – farming

Summary

Italy is a beautiful country with a long and interesting history. Italians have developed their own customs and way of life.

143

How developed is Italy?

All countries are different. Some, like the UK, are wealthy and have high **standards of living**. They are said to be **developed**. Others, like Kenya for example, are poor. They have low standards of living and are said to be **developing**.

Measuring development can be difficult. The most commonly used method is to look at wealth. This can be misleading, however, as even in the richest countries there are people living in bad conditions with little money. A better measure is **quality of life**. This takes into account how happy and content people are.

Look carefully at the graphs below. Notice that Italy is very similar to the UK. Both are developed countries.

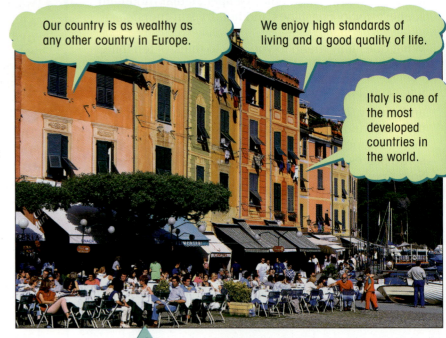

Our country is as wealthy as any other country in Europe.

We enjoy high standards of living and a good quality of life.

Italy is one of the most developed countries in the world.

A

B

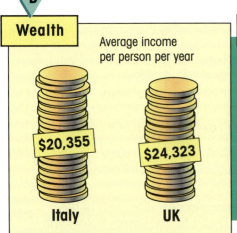

Wealth

Average income per person per year

$20,355 — Italy

$24,323 — UK

Health

Number of people per doctor

211 — Italy

300 — UK

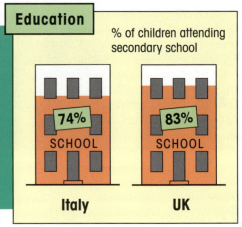

Education

% of children attending secondary school

74% — Italy

83% — UK

Activities

1 Match the following beginnings with the correct endings.

Beginnings	Endings
Development is	a high standard of living
A developed country has	of how happy and contented people are
A developing country has	about growth and progress
Standard of living is a measure	a low standard of living
Quality of life is a measure	of how well off a person or country is

2 Look at graphs **B** above. Give three reasons why Italy can be described as a developed country.

Italy only became a single nation in 1861. Until then it was made up of several small states, each with its own government and way of life. Even today there are big differences between parts of Italy. The biggest differences are between the North and the South.

The people in the North are much richer than those in the South. Their region has modern industry and uses the latest farming methods. The South is less well developed. Many people there live in difficult conditions. Progress is being made but there is still much to do.

C The North and South compared

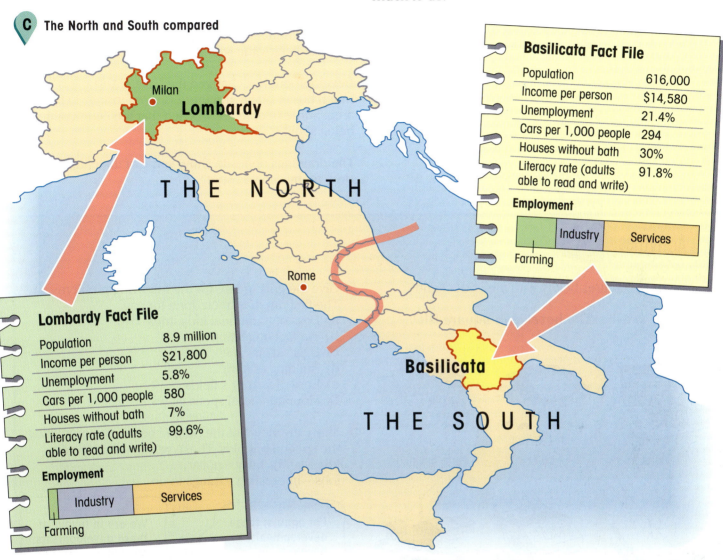

Basilicata Fact File

Population	616,000
Income per person	$14,580
Unemployment	21.4%
Cars per 1,000 people	294
Houses without bath	30%
Literacy rate (adults able to read and write)	91.8%

Employment

Farming | Industry | Services

Lombardy Fact File

Population	8.9 million
Income per person	$21,800
Unemployment	5.8%
Cars per 1,000 people	580
Houses without bath	7%
Literacy rate (adults able to read and write)	99.6%

Employment

Farming | Industry | Services

3 Look at map **C** above for this activity. Write either **North** or **South** to complete these sentences.

a) Lombardy is in the ....
b) Basilicata is in the ......
c) The richest area is the ......
d) The best chance of a job is in the ......
e) The worst housing conditions are in the ......
f) Fewer people can read and write in the ......
g) Most jobs are in industry and services in the ......
h) Farming is more important in the ......

D

Our country is developed, but that doesn't mean we're all well off.

Summary Italy is one of the most developed countries in the world. However, development is not spread evenly.

How is the Valle d'Aosta changing?

The Valle d'Aosta is in the Alps in north-west Italy. It is a beautiful area with steep-sided valleys, fast-flowing rivers and pretty villages. Some of Europe's highest mountains may be found there. They are snow-covered throughout the year.

Until recently, the Valle d'Aosta was a quiet place. There were few good roads and most people worked on farms or in the forests. There was a little industry in the small villages scattered along the valley floor.

The area is very different now. It is developing as a major holiday area. Ski-ing, climbing and walking are the main attractions. Other visitors go there simply to relax and enjoy the scenery.

Development has changed the Valle d'Aosta. It is now a much busier place and there is more money in the area. Some people are worried that the countryside is being spoilt.

The drawings opposite show some of the changes. How many can you spot?

Activities

1 Match the features below with the correct grid squares.
Answer like this: **The hotel is in square D10.**

Hotel

Dairy   Farm buildings

Ski lift

Ski factory

Ski station

2 Copy and complete these sentences to show how land use has changed in the area. The first one has been done for you.
a) Forest (F3) changed to **ski slope** (F8)
b) Dairy (B5) changed to ...... (B10)
c) Farm buildings (D5) changed to ...... (D10)
d) Farmland (A3) changed to ...... (A8)
e) Narrow road (C5) changed to ...... (C10)
f) Winding river (F4) changed to ...... (F9)

3 Give three other changes in the area. Answer in the same way as you did for activity **1**.

4 Give the grid square for the following problems. The first one has been done for you.
a) Loss of traditional industries   B10
b) Traffic congestion ...
c) Ugly ski lifts ...
d) Building of dam ...
e) Loss of farmer's fields ...
f) Mountain hotel spoils views ...

5 Show the views of the people below by completing the speech bubbles. These words will help you:
lost – land – busy – noisy
jobs – interesting – things to do

I'm against these developments because ...... and ......

We are in favour of these developments because ...... and ......

Local farmer   Teenagers about to leave school

Summary   The Valle d'Aosta has become popular with tourists. This has brought many benefits but has also caused problems.

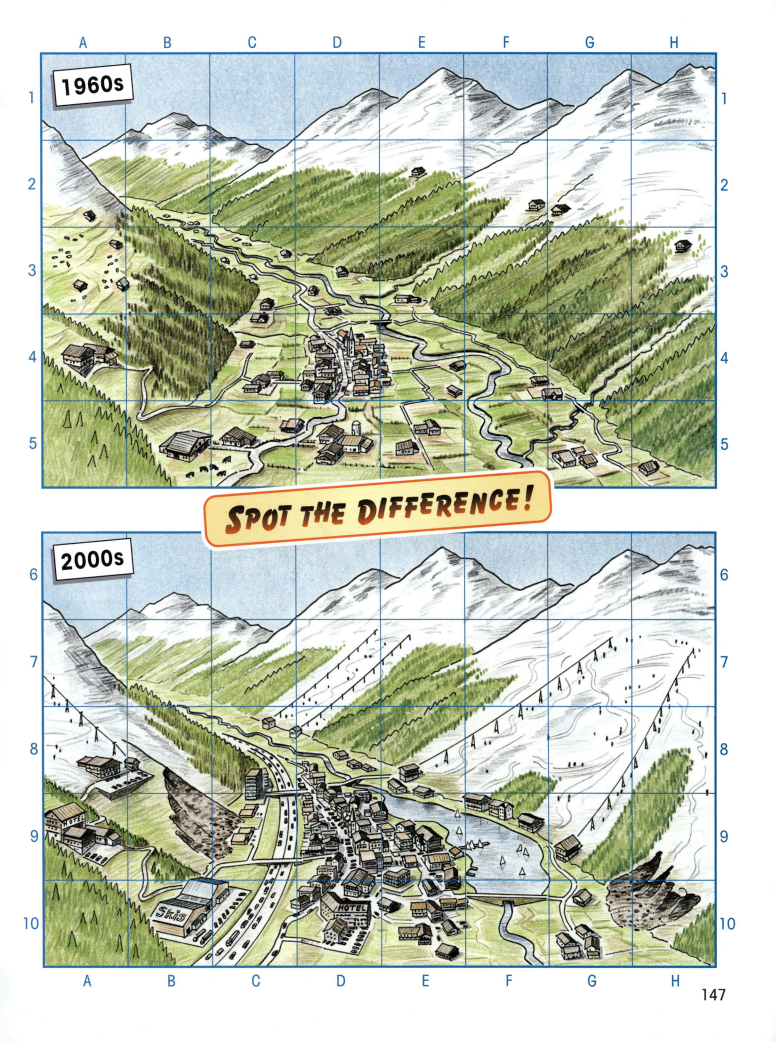

SPOT THE DIFFERENCE!

What is the North Italian Plain like?

The North Italian Plain lies between the Alps in the north and the Apennines in the south. It is Italy's largest area of lowland.

The area is also the country's richest region. This is because it has Italy's best farmland, its best energy supplies and most important industries.

At the western end of the plain is an area called the 'Industrial Triangle'. Three great cities, Milan, Turin and Genoa, lie at the corners of the 'Triangle'.

Industrial growth has been very rapid here. Fiat and Iveco (vehicle makers), Zanussi and Benetton are some of the famous companies that have factories in the area.

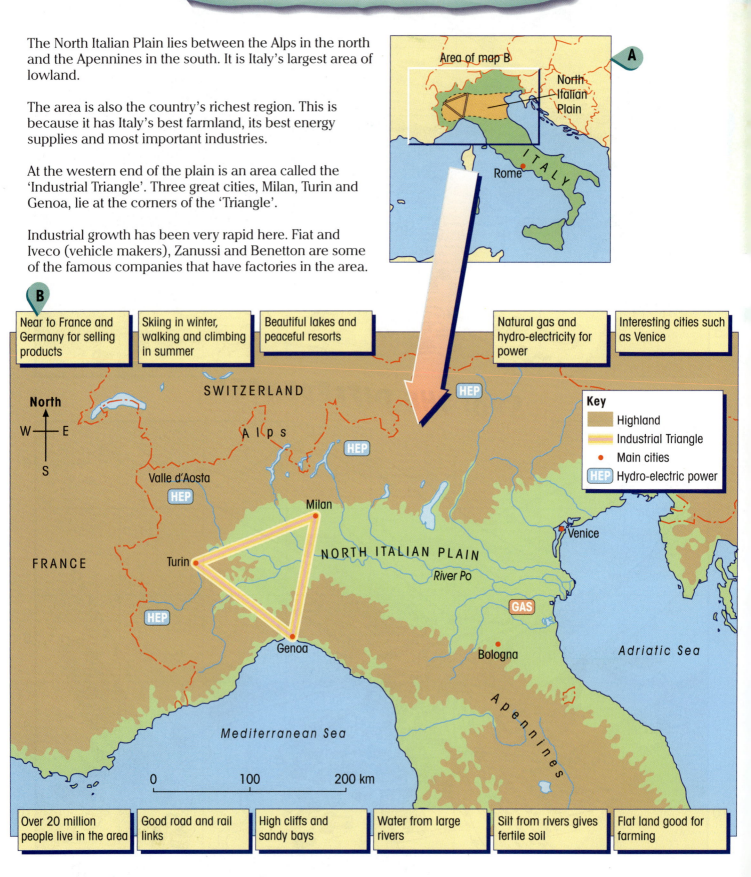

A Area of map B — North Italian Plain — ITALY — Rome

B

Near to France and Germany for selling products

Skiing in winter, walking and climbing in summer

Beautiful lakes and peaceful resorts

Natural gas and hydro-electricity for power

Interesting cities such as Venice

SWITZERLAND

North — W–E — S

A l p s

Valle d'Aosta

HEP

Milan

NORTH ITALIAN PLAIN

River Po

Venice

FRANCE

Turin

HEP

GAS

Genoa

Bologna

Adriatic Sea

A p e n n i n e s

Mediterranean Sea

0   100   200 km

Key
- Highland
- Industrial Triangle
- • Main cities
- HEP Hydro-electric power

Over 20 million people live in the area

Good road and rail links

High cliffs and sandy bays

Water from large rivers

Silt from rivers gives fertile soil

Flat land good for farming

C Picking tomatoes on the North Italian Plain

D The Fiat factory near Turin

Activities

Activities 1 to 13 are about the North Italian Plain. Choose your answer or answers from the boxes.

1 Which range of mountains lie to the north?

| Pennines | Apennines | Valle d'Aosta | Alps |

2 Which highland area lies to the south?

| Pennines | Apennines | Valle d'Aosta | Alps |

3 Which cities make up the Industrial Triangle?

| Milan | Venice | Genoa | Turin |

4 Which city is on the Mediterranean Sea?

| Milan | Venice | Genoa | Turin |

5 What is the distance from Turin to Venice?

| 120 | 234 | 390 | 682 | km

6 What is the distance from Milan to Genoa?

| 120 | 234 | 390 | 682 | km

7 Which river flows across the plain?

| Milan | Pie | Po | Como |

8 What two types of energy supply are there?

| coal | gas | hydro-electricity | oil |

9 Which two countries lie next to Italy?

| Britain | France | Germany | Switzerland |

10 What three things help to make the area wealthy?

| farming | skiing | energy | industry |

11 What two things make farming good in the area?

| dry climate | flat land | fertile soil | mountains |

12 Which two vehicle producers are in the area?

| Nissan | Toyota | Fiat | Iveco |

13 Where has industrial growth been most rapid?

| Valle d'Aosta | Venice | Industrial Triangle | Alps |

14 **a)** Write sentences to describe each of the photos **C** and **D**. The words below will help you.

b) Give each description a title.

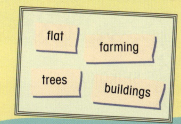

flat
farming
trees
buildings

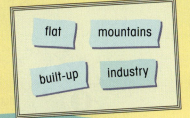

flat
mountains
built-up
industry

Summary The North Italian Plain is Italy's wealthiest region. It has the country's best farmland and most modern industries.

16 Japan

What are Japan's main features?

Japan lies off the east coast of Asia in the Pacific Ocean. It is made up of four large islands and over 1,000 smaller ones. The islands were formed by volcanoes, many of which are still active.

The volcanoes and earthquakes, which often happen here, are caused by the movement of giant **plates** on the Earth's surface. Japan lies at the point where four of these plates meet.

Almost 90 per cent of the land is covered by mountains. Short but fast-flowing rivers flow from the mountains down to the sea.

There is very little flat land. Most of it is near the sea. Almost all of the population is squeezed into these coastal areas. They are amongst the most crowded places in the world.

B Mount Fuji is Japan's highest mountain and most famous volcano. Over half a million people climb it every year.

HOKKAIDO

C

Sapporo

Sea of Japan

North

W — E

S

HONSHU

Pacific Ocean

Kyoto

Tokyo

Kobe

D

B

Hiroshima

Mount Fuji

Mount Unzen

Osaka

SHIKOKU

E

Mount Aso

KYUSHU

Kagoshima

0   300 km

Key

	Highland
	Lowland
●	Main cities
	Volcano
C	Photo location

150

C The north has very cold winters with heavy snowfalls. Snow festivals are held where giant sculptures are carved out of ice.

D The Kobe earthquake of 1995 left 5,000 people dead, 10,000 injured and 250,000 homeless.

E

The south is warm and wet. The area has tropical plants and attractive countryside. There are **coral reefs** along the coast, and spectacular volcanoes.

Activities

1 Complete these ten sentences.
 a) The biggest island is ......
 b) The most northerly island is ......
 c) The other two main islands are ......
 d) The length of Japan from north to south is ......
 e) The width of Honshu near Tokyo is ......
 f) The coldest part of Japan is ......
 g) The highest volcano is ......
 h) Japan has volcanoes and earthquakes because ......
 i) The area where most people live is ......
 j) Places in Japan are very crowded because ......

2 a) Give each of the photos **B**, **C**, **D** and **E** a title.
 b) Match the words below with each one.
 c) Add two extra words for each photo.

Answer like this:
A = Mount Fuji = cone-shaped, ...

- cone-shaped   - festival
- warm weather   - sculpture
- steep-sided   - fine scenery
- shaken   - coast
- snow-capped   - disaster
- cold   - destroyed

Summary

Japan is made up of volcanic islands. Most of the country is mountainous with few people. The coastal regions have huge cities and are very crowded. The Japanese people live a modern life but are proud of their traditions.

How developed is Japan?

Japan is one of the wealthiest and most modern countries in the world. Its success is due mainly to industrial growth. Goods made in Japan are sold all around the world. The companies that make the goods have become rich and are able to pay their workers good wages.

This has helped Japanese people enjoy a high standard of living. They have money to spend on food, education and health care. They can also afford to buy their own cars and expensive household goods like television sets, video recorders and computers.

All of these things help make Japan a **developed country**. A developed country is one that is rich, has many services and a high standard of living.

A Some famous Japanese companies

B

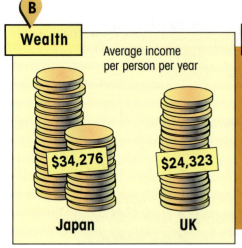

Wealth

Average income per person per year

$34,276 — Japan

$24,323 — UK

Health

Number of people per doctor

600 — Japan

300 — UK

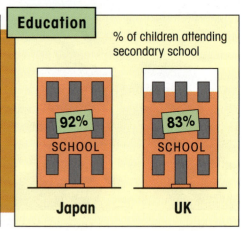

Education

% of children attending secondary school

92% — Japan — SCHOOL

83% — UK — SCHOOL

Activities

1 Complete these sentences using words from the spiral. The words read out from the centre.

a) Japan is a country that is ......
b) Japan's success is due to ......
c) Japanese people enjoy a high ......
d) The Japanese have good ......
e) Most Japanese people can afford ......
f) A Japanese car maker is ......
g) A Japanese electronics company is ......
h) Almost all children in Japan go to ......

C

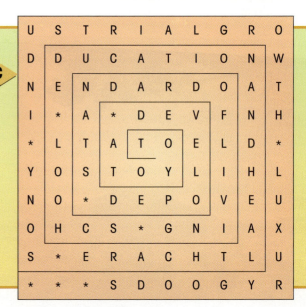

Not everything is perfect in Japan, however. Many people are unhappy with their way of life. Others are worried about how industrial developments are damaging the countryside.

People want future growth in Japan to be **sustainable**. That means it must not threaten ways of life or damage the environment. It must be sensible development.

D Development: the good and the bad

Our **cities are busy and crowded**. We have very little space to live in.

Our **countryside is protected** and well looked after.

We have **very little crime** in Japan.

We **work long hours** and have very short holidays.

School is very hard. We work five days a week, some evenings and often on Saturdays.

There are **plenty of jobs** here. Hardly anyone is out of work.

Some of us are poor and have a difficult life.

We use the **latest technology** to make life easy.

Development should help us today but must not damage the future.

2 Make a copy of table **E** below. Sort the statements from photo **D** into the correct columns. You need only write the words in **bold**.

E	Development in Japan	
	The Good	The Bad

3 Make a list of as many Japanese companies as you can. Try to get at least fifteen. Say what each one makes.

Summary Japan is one of the world's richest countries. Most of its people have a high standard of living and a good quality of life.

What is Tokyo like?

Tokyo is a huge city. It stretches for almost 100 km along Japan's east coast and has an estimated population of 12 million. A further 32 million people live in the surrounding area. Tokyo is one of the largest cities in the world.

The city is incredibly crowded and busy. The main centre covers a large area and has little open space. There are many smaller centres, each with its own shops, offices, factories, houses, shrines and parks. Most of them also have a railway station.

Many streets have no names, and houses are often numbered in the order they are built in. Finding your way around can be very difficult!

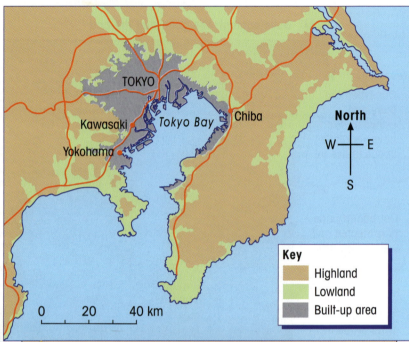

Key
■ Highland
■ Lowland
■ Built-up area

0   20   40 km

A Tokyo began as a small settlement on Tokyo Bay. Here there was plenty of flat land and a good sheltered harbour for ships. Water was available from nearby rivers.

B Tokyo is Japan's capital and financial centre. Most of the world's largest companies have offices in the city. The central area has many tall buildings. They are mainly banks, offices and government buildings.

C Tokyo is one of the world's best shopping cities. There is also a huge variety of hotels, restaurants and places of entertainment. Roads and railways from all over Japan meet in Tokyo.

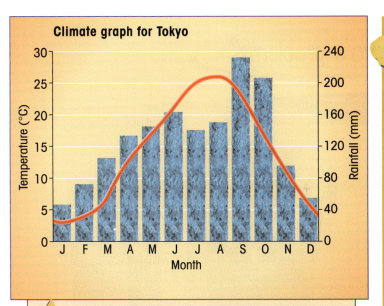

Climate graph for Tokyo

D Tokyo can be very wet. It has more than twice as much rainfall as London. The summers are hot and humid. Winters are cool but drier. From June to October the city may be hit by **tropical storms**. These bring hurricane-force winds and torrential rain.

E Tokyo is a major industrial centre. The smaller factories are mostly mixed in with offices, shops and housing. Larger factories are built on **reclaimed** land in Tokyo Bay. The city is also an important port.

Activities

1 Use map **A** to do this activity. Copy the sentences below and write **true** or **false** beside each one.

a) Tokyo Bay is 80 km wide.
b) Chiba is about 40 km from Tokyo.
c) Tokyo is on the west side of Tokyo Bay.
d) Yokohama is north of Tokyo.
e) Tokyo has a deep, sheltered harbour.
f) Tokyo lies on a large area of flat land.

2 Complete these sentences using graph **D**.

a) The highest temperature is ......
b) The lowest temperature is ......
c) The three warmest months are ......
d) The three coldest months are ......
e) The two wettest months are ......
f) The two driest months are ......
g) The months with more than 100 mm of rain are ......

3 Match each of the labels in the drawing below with a letter from photo **E**.
Answer like this: A = Tokyo

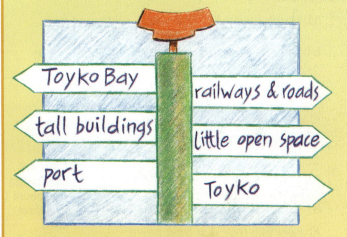

Toyko Bay
tall buildings
port
railways & roads
little open space
Toyko

4 Copy and complete the following four sentences using the words in the drawing above.

● The city of .... is located on ....
● It has many .... and ....
● .... from all over the country meet in Tokyo.
● The city is Japan's capital and an important ....

Summary Tokyo is Japan's capital and most important city. It is one of the world's largest and busiest cities.

What are Tokyo's problems?

Tokyo is one of the busiest and most crowded cities in the world. Its well-paid jobs and exciting lifestyle have attracted large numbers of people from surrounding areas.

However, the city's huge size has led to many problems. These include overcrowding, a strain on transport systems, and pollution.

There is also the problem of **natural hazards**. Tokyo lies in an earthquake area and is also affected by powerful tropical storms called **cyclones**.

A

Tokyo's overcrowded railways

Activities

1 a) Match photo **A** above with a comment from storyboard **D** opposite.
  b) Which of the words below help describe the photo? Put them into a sentence.

- buses
- trains
- crowded
- empty
- quiet
- busy
- pushers
- pullers

2 a) Which comments are good news?
  b) Which comments are bad news?

Answer like this: **1 = bad news**

** You will need to use storyboard **D** to answer these activities.*

3 Make a copy of table **B** below. Sort the comments into the correct columns. You need only write the number for each one. Some comments may be used more than once. Some are not problems so won't be used at all.

B

Tokyo's problems			
Lack of space	Earthquakes	Travel	Pollution

4 The people in **C** below have problems in Tokyo. Copy and complete the sentences for each one.

C

I want to build a new shop in the centre of Tokyo. This is difficult because................ and....................................

I travel into the city each day for work. This is difficult because....... and......................

We want to live in Tokyo but are not happy because the houses are.................... We are also frightened of......

Summary Tokyo's rapid growth has caused many problems. These include a lack of space, congestion and pollution.

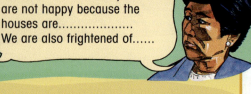

D **Storyboard: Some problems of Tokyo's growth**

1 There's just no space left in our city.

2 Building land is the most expensive in the world.

3 Our houses are tiny and lack gardens.

4 There are hardly any parks for fresh air and relaxation.

5 But we have modern buildings and plenty to do.

6 Tokyo is always crowded and busy.

7 The traffic in the centre is terrible.

8 But we have one of the world's best transport systems.

9 Two million people travel to the city each day for work.

10 'Pushers' are used to cram people into trains.

11 Earthquakes are common here.

12 A big one in 1923 killed 140,000 people.

13 We expect another big one very soon.

14 Our buildings are now made earthquake-proof.

15 There's plenty of work in Tokyo ...

16 ... but the city is noisy and dirty.

17 Traffic and factories cause most pollution.

18 Waste is dumped in the sea to make more land.

19 The air is cleaner now than it used to be.

How developed are we?

All countries are different. Some are rich and have high **standards of living**. Others are poor and have lower standards of living.

Development is a measure of how rich or how poor a country is. Rich countries are said to be **developed**. Poor countries are said to be **developing**.

Notice on map **A** that the richer countries are mainly in the 'North' and the poorer countries are in the 'South'.

Activities

1 Match the following clues with the crossword answers. All of the answers can be found on these two pages.
Answer like this: **a)** = Rich = 12

a)	Developed countries are this
b)	River that flows through Egypt
c)	Brazilian river
d)	River in the USA
e)	Ocean east of Africa
f)	Country with poorest education
g)	Wealthiest country
h)	Country with best health care
i)	Poor country in South America
j)	Capital city of Japan
k)	The United Kingdom's main city
l)	Capital city almost on the Equator
m)	Part of the world that is rich
n)	Part of the world that is poor
o)	Less developed countries are this
p)	A measure of how rich or poor a country is

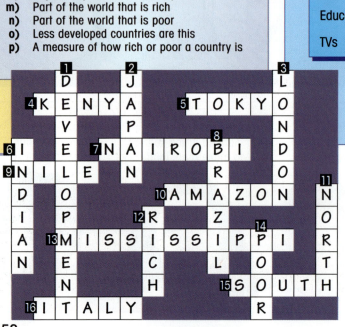

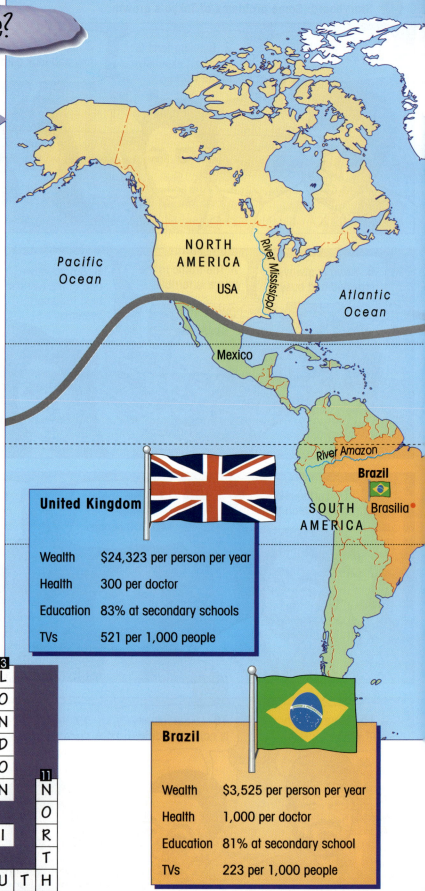

A

NORTH AMERICA

Pacific Ocean

USA

River Mississippi

Atlantic Ocean

Mexico

River Amazon

Brazil

SOUTH AMERICA

Brasilia

United Kingdom

Wealth	$24,323 per person per year
Health	300 per doctor
Education	83% at secondary schools
TVs	521 per 1,000 people

Brazil

Wealth	$3,525 per person per year
Health	1,000 per doctor
Education	81% at secondary school
TVs	223 per 1,000 people

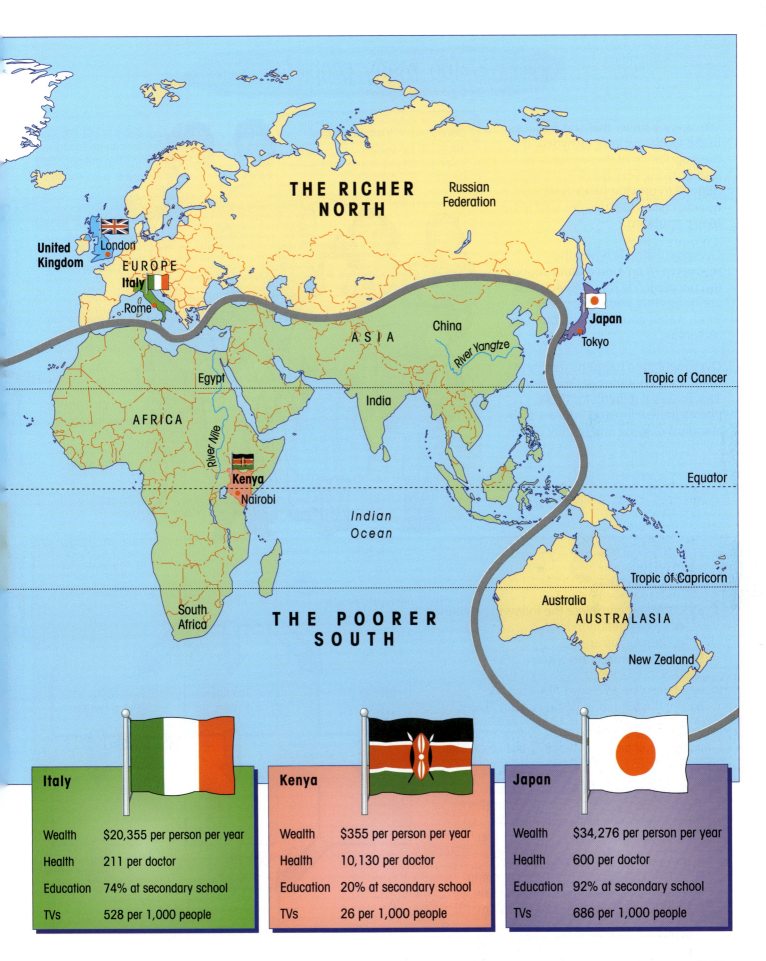

THE RICHER NORTH

Russian Federation

United Kingdom

London

EUROPE

Italy

Rome

ASIA

China

River Yangtze

Japan

Tokyo

Tropic of Cancer

Egypt

AFRICA

River Nile

India

Kenya

Nairobi

Indian Ocean

Equator

South Africa

THE POORER SOUTH

Australia

AUSTRALASIA

Tropic of Capricorn

New Zealand

Italy

Wealth	$20,355 per person per year
Health	211 per doctor
Education	74% at secondary school
TVs	528 per 1,000 people

Kenya

Wealth	$355 per person per year
Health	10,130 per doctor
Education	20% at secondary school
TVs	26 per 1,000 people

Japan

Wealth	$34,276 per person per year
Health	600 per doctor
Education	92% at secondary school
TVs	686 per 1,000 people

Too many people?

We already know that some places in the world are very crowded. If the population of these places is also growing very quickly, it can be difficult to provide for everyone's needs. Places like this are said to be **overpopulated**.

Overpopulation is when the resources of an area cannot support the people living there. **Resources** are things that people need, like food, water, good soil, and building materials.

Overpopulation happens mainly in the poorer countries of the world. This makes it difficult for these places to develop and improve their standard of living and quality of life.

Development is about making life better for people ....but overpopulation makes development difficult.

There is not enough food to go round ... . so many people are in poor health.

There are not enough jobs for people ....so we have very little money......

...and can't afford good health care, education or housing.

This all means we have low standards of living ... ... and a poor quality of life.

A

Activities

1 a) Copy and complete the following sentences.
  ● Overpopulation is ......
  ● Resources are ......
b) List six different resources.

2 a) Make a larger copy of diagram **B**.
b) Put the following in the correct boxes.

| Homeless families | Shortage of money | Poor health | Poor education and health care |

3 Look at photos **C**, **D**, **E** and **F**, which show some problems in poor countries. Write a sentence to describe each photo. The words below will help you.

C people – thin – starving – help
D sad – clothing – no money – begging
E child – sick – starving – health care
F family – homeless – railway – slum

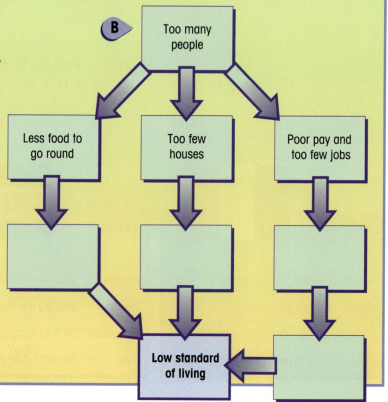

B

Too many people

Less food to go round

Too few houses

Poor pay and too few jobs

Low standard of living

C Sudan – waiting for food at a food distribution centre

D Street beggar – Calcutta, India

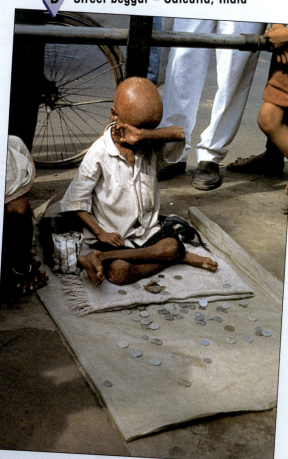

E Emergency medical aid – Rwanda

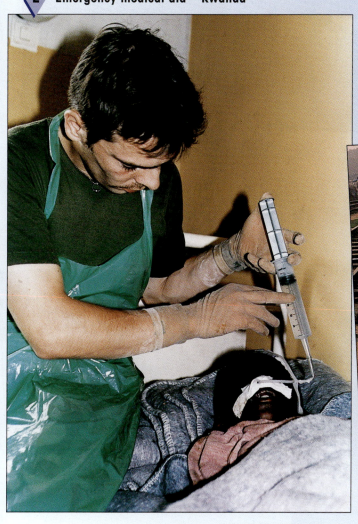

F Homeless families – Dhaka, Bangladesh

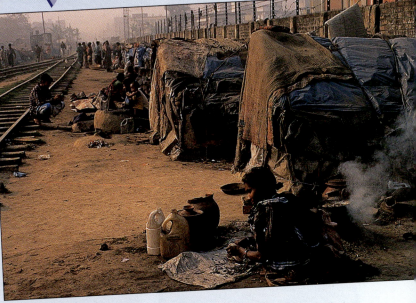

Summary Some countries are crowded and have a rapid population growth. This can cause problems for people and slow down development.

How do jobs affect development?

Work in the poorer countries of the world can be very different from the UK. Most people there work long hours and earn little money. Few people, especially away from the city, have a proper full-time job.

Informal sector work is a feature of these countries. This is where people hunt around and do anything to earn some money and help each other out. Many of the jobs are done by hand because there is a lack of modern tools and machinery.

Waste materials are often **recycled** and, by the skill of the worker, made into useful and saleable products.

Most businesses in poorer countries are small-scale. Wood-carving, pottery-making and weaving are typical of these. They are often run by families.

The photos below show some people at work in the less developed world.

A

B

C

D

E

F

The jobs people do can be divided into three main types. As drawing **G** shows, these are **primary**, **secondary** and **tertiary** (see pages 74 and 75).

Poorer, less developed countries have most workers in primary industries. These include farming, forestry and mining, which make little money.

A country begins to develop when its secondary and tertiary industries start to grow. Poor countries have to struggle to develop these industries. This is usually because they can't afford the factories and machinery that are needed.

Sometimes big companies like Ford or Coca-Cola set up a factory and employ local people. This can bring wealth to an area and help it to develop.

G

TYPES OF WORK

Primary industries provide basic materials like food, coal and timber.

Secondary industries make things.

Tertiary industries give help to others. They provide a service.

H

Employment structures

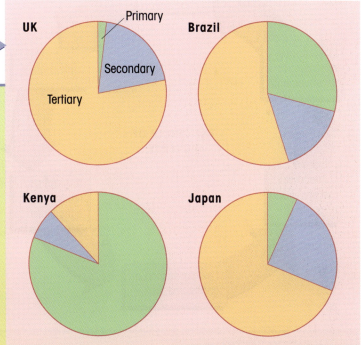

Activities

1 Match the photos **A**, **B**, **C**, **D**, **E** and **F** with the following headings.
Answer like this: A = _Wood-carving in Kenya_

- Shoe-shining in Ethiopia
- Fishing in Sri Lanka
- Weaving a carpet in India
- Farming in the Philippines
- Selling goods in a market, Guatemala

2 What type of job (primary, secondary or tertiary) is being done in each photo?
Answer like this: A = _secondary_

3 Use the pie graphs **H** to answer this activity. Copy and complete the table below. Use the following figures:

2 7 12 16 24 55 69 81

Country	Primary	Secondary	Tertiary
UK		20	78
Brazil	29		
Kenya		7	
Japan			

4 Complete these sentences using information from pie graphs **H** and your completed table from activity **3**.
a) The country with most primary jobs is ......
b) The country with fewest primary jobs is ......
c) The country with most tertiary jobs is ......
d) The country with fewest secondary jobs is ......
e) The country that is least developed is ......
f) The two countries that are likely to be wealthiest are ......

Summary
The type of work done in a country affects its level of development. Poor countries have a larger primary workforce than rich countries.

What affects development?

Development is about progress and improving the quality of life for people. Improving conditions in the poorer countries of the world can be difficult, however. The main problem is a lack of money.

As diagram **A** shows, the lack of money makes it almost impossible to build up industry and modernise farming. Without this, the country cannot develop or improve conditions for its people.

To make progress, most poorer countries have to rely on help from richer countries. One way that help can be given is through aid schemes.

Aid can be in the form of grants, loans and technical help. It comes from governments, international organisations and charities such as Oxfam and Christian Aid. Diagram **B** shows how aid can help a country develop and improve its standard of living.

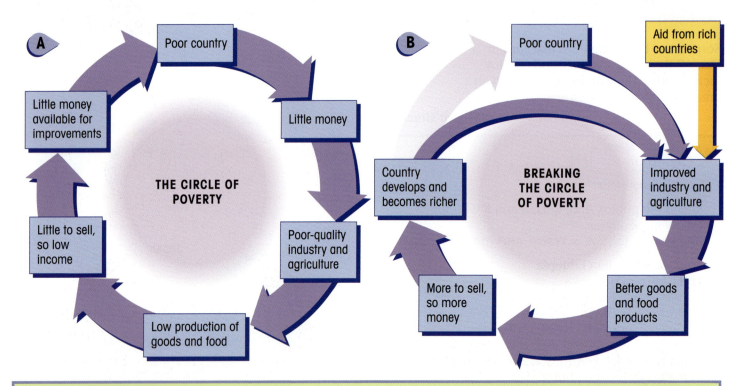

A THE CIRCLE OF POVERTY

Poor country → Little money → Poor-quality industry and agriculture → Low production of goods and food → Little to sell, so low income → Little money available for improvements → Poor country

B BREAKING THE CIRCLE OF POVERTY

Aid from rich countries → Improved industry and agriculture → Better goods and food products → More to sell, so more money → Country develops and becomes richer → Poor country

Activities

1 Look carefully at the snakes and ladders game opposite. List the statements that are **problems** for development.
Answer like this: **Problem = 46**

2 **a)** Make a copy of table **C**.
b) Put each of the **aid** statements from the game into the correct column. You need only give the square number. One has been done for you.

3 With a partner, play the snakes and ladders game. The winner is the first to reach the end with the exact number.

Use two coins for your moves:
● Head then a tail = 1 move
● Tail then a head = 2 moves
● Two tails = 3 moves
● Two heads = 4 moves

C

Aid for development		
Countries	Organisations	Charities
	43	

Summary
It is difficult for poorer countries to improve their standard of living. Aid is a form of help usually given by wealthy areas of the world to the poorer areas.

The way to development

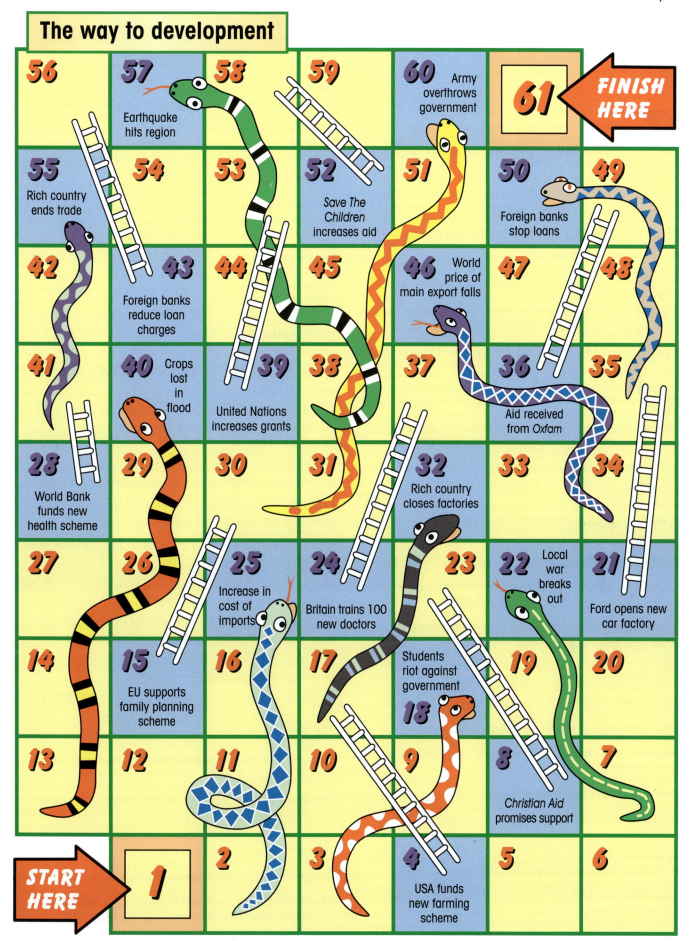

56

57 Earthquake hits region

58

59

60 Army overthrows government

61 FINISH HERE

55 Rich country ends trade

54

53

52 Save The Children increases aid

51

50 Foreign banks stop loans

49

42

43 Foreign banks reduce loan charges

44

45

46 World price of main export falls

47

48

41

40 Crops lost in flood

39 United Nations increases grants

38

37

36 Aid received from Oxfam

35

28 World Bank funds new health scheme

29

30

31

32 Rich country closes factories

33

34

27

26

25 Increase in cost of imports

24 Britain trains 100 new doctors

23

22 Local war breaks out

21 Ford opens new car factory

14

15 EU supports family planning scheme

16

17

Students riot against government

19

20

13

12

11

10

18

9

8 Christian Aid promises support

7

START HERE

1

2

3

4 USA funds new farming scheme

5

6

Glossary

Agriculture The growing of crops and rearing of animals. *64*

Aid Help usually given by the richer countries of the world to the poorer ones. *164, 165*

Annual rainfall The amount of rain that falls in a year. *8*

Birth rate The number of people being born in one year for each 1,000 of the population. *97, 98*

By-pass A road built around a busy area to avoid traffic jams. *40, 41, 42, 43*

Canopy An almost unbroken top layer of trees which act like a roof over the tropical rainforest. *118*

Central Business District (CBD) The middle of a town or city where most shops and offices are found. *26, 27, 29*

Climate The average weather conditions of a place. *4, 112, 113*

Conflict Disagreement over something. *32, 33, 42*

Congestion charging A payment introduced for motorists using London city centre. *37*

Conservation Protecting and preserving animals, plants, buildings and the environment. *87*

Coral A type of limestone rock made up of the skeletons of marine creatures. *151*

Coral reef A band of coral lying off the coast. *151*

Core The central part of the Earth. *124*

Country Code A set of rules that helps protect the countryside. *86*

Crust The outer layer of the Earth. *124*

Death rate The number of people dying in one year per 1,000 of the population. *97, 98*

Deforestation The clearing and destruction of forests. *15*

Deposition The laying down of material carried by rivers, sea, ice or wind. *58, 59*

Developed country A country that has a lot of money, many services and a higher standard of living. *46, 106, 144, 152, 153, 158*

Developing country A country that is often quite poor, has few services and a lower standard of living. *106, 144, 158*

Development How rich or poor a country is compared with others. *47, 106, 158*

Earthquake A movement or tremor of the Earth's crust. *125, 150, 151*

Economic activity A primary, secondary or tertiary industry. *64, 74*

Employment structure The proportion of people working in primary, secondary and tertiary activities. *163*

Environment The natural or physical surroundings where people, animals and plants live. *70, 90–93*

Equator An imaginary line around the Earth halfway between the north and south poles. *104*

Equatorial climate Places near to the Equator which are hot and wet all year. *116*

Erosion The wearing away and removal of rock, soil, etc. by rivers, sea, ice and wind. *58, 59*

European Union (EU) A group of European countries working together for the benefit of everyone. *46*

Evergreen Plants that always have some green leaves growing throughout the year. *119*

Exports Goods sold to other countries. *76, 77, 110*

Flood When water overflows and covers an area. *14–23, 56, 58, 62, 63*

Flood plain The flat area at the bottom of a valley which is often flooded. *14, 55*

Gorge A steep-sided valley. *60, 61*

Grid references A group of four or six figures used to find a place on an Ordnance Survey map. *28*

High-tech industries Industries using advanced machines, e.g. computers, and skilled people. *47, 143*

Human features Features that are a result of action by people. *16, 67, 90, 112*

Industry Where people work. *64, 74*

Informal work Employment that is not permanent, regular or properly organised. *162*

Inner city An area of factories and old houses next to the city centre. *26, 27*

Inner suburbs An area of housing close to the city centre. *26, 27*

Landforms The shape of the land. *54, 55*

Land use Describes how the land in towns or the countryside is used. It includes housing, industry and farming. *26, 27*

Lava Molten rock flowing out of the ground, usually from volcanoes. *126, 127*

Load The material carried by a river. *58*

Location factors Things to consider when choosing a site for something. *80, 81*

Managed The way something is carefully looked after. *87*

Mantle The layer of the Earth below the crust and above the core. *124*

Manufacturing An industry where something is made. Also called a secondary industry. *74*

Market A place where raw materials and goods are sold. A group of people who buy raw materials or goods. *80, 81*

Meander A large bend in a river. *55, 59*

Migrants People who move from one place to live or work in another. *98–103, 109*

Migration The movement of people from one place to another to live or to work. *98–103*

Mild Not too cold. *7*

National Park An area of beautiful countryside preserved by law from development. *87, 88, 89, 104*

Natural habitat The natural home of plants and animals. *70*

Natural hazard A great force of nature such as an earthquake or volcano which is a danger to people. *156*

Natural resources Raw materials that are obtained from the environment, e.g. water, coal and soil. *64, 74*

North Atlantic Drift A warm ocean current that brings mild conditions to the west of Britain in winter. *7*

Ordnance Survey The official government organisation responsible for producing maps in the UK. *28, 29, 48–51, 56, 57, 78, 79*

Outer suburbs The newest part of the town on the edge of the city. *26, 27*

Overpopulated When there are more people living in an area than the area can support. *160*

Physical environment The Earth's natural features such as mountains, rivers, volcanoes and earthquakes. *90, 91*

Physical features Natural features that include relief, drainage and vegetation. *66, 112*

Plate boundary The place where plates meet. *124, 125*

Plates Large sections of the Earth's crust. *124, 125, 150*

Plunge pool A hollow at the base of a waterfall caused by erosion. *60, 61*

Population distribution How people are spread out over an area. *94*

Population explosion A sudden rapid rise in the number of people. *96*

Population growth The increase in the number of people in an area. *96, 97*

Precipitation Water falling from the sky. It includes rain, snow, sleet and hail. *12*

Primary activity Collecting and using natural resources, e.g. farming, fishing, forestry and mining. *64, 74, 75, 163*

Pull factors Things that attract people to live in an area. *98, 99*

Push factors Things that make people want to leave an area. *98, 99*

Quality of life How content people are with their lives and the environment in which they live. *32, 42, 96, 106, 144*

Rainfall distribution How rainfall is spread out over an area. *8*

Raw materials Natural resources that are used to make things. *64, 80*

Reclaimed land Land that has been recovered and can be put to some use. *155*

Recycled Goods that are made from materials that have been used before. 162

Redevelopment The rebuilding of an area for a new use. *48*

Relief rain Rain caused by air being forced to rise over hills and mountains. *9*

Reservoir An artificial lake. *56*

Resources Things that can be useful to people. They can be natural, like iron and coal, or of other value, like money and skilled workers. *160*

Rural An area of land that is mainly countryside. *50*

Rural-to-urban migration The movement of people from the countryside to the towns and cities. *98*

Safari The name given to a type of holiday where wild animals are viewed in their natural surroundings. *104*

Secondary activities Where natural resources are turned into goods which we can use. *74, 75, 163*

Settlement A place where people live. *24, 112*

Shanty town A collection of shacks and poor-quality housing which often lack electricity, a water supply and means of sewage disposal. *108, 109*

Site The actual place where a settlement or industry first grew up. *24, 80*

Standard of living How well-off a country or person is. *46, 106, 134, 144, 158*

Temperature A measure of how warm or how cold it is. *6, 7, 12, 13*

Tertiary activities An industry that provides a service for people. Teachers, shop assistants and tourist industry workers are in this type of industry. *74, 132, 133, 163*

Tourists People who travel to places for recreation and leisure. *47, 50, 132*

Trade The exchange of goods between people or countries. *77*

Transportation The movement of eroded material by rivers, sea, ice and wind. *58*

Tropical rainforests Tall, dense forests found in hot, wet climates. *114–121*

Tropical storm A weather system with very strong winds and heavy rain. *155*

Urban An area of land that is mainly covered in buildings. *34, 26, 27*

Urban model The pattern of land use in a town. *26, 27*

Urbanisation The growing proportion of people living in urban areas. *15*

Vegetation The plant life of an area. *112, 113, 114*

Visibility The distance that can be seen. *12*

Volcano A cone-shaped mountain or hill often made up from lava and ash. *125–131, 150*

Waterfall A sudden fall of water over a steep drop. *55, 60, 61*

Weather The day-to-day condition of the atmosphere. It includes temperature, rainfall and wind. *4, 6*

Wildlife The animals of an area. This could include birds, insects, fish and other animals. *114–115*

Work Something people do to earn a living. 64, 74, 112, 113

Writing frame An aid that helps us plan and structure a piece of writing. *42, 43, 92, 93*

Zones Areas with similar features. *26, 27*